Pokémon

TRADING CARD GAME

The Official Nintendo Player's Guide

CONTENTS

This guide builds your Pokémon Trading Card Game knowledge in three ways. The Master the Basics section gives a rundown of the game's rules and basic strategy. The Challenge the Masters section deals with the eight Clubs and Club Masters. Finally, learn detailed information about the cards and decks in the Deck Data section.

MASTER THE BASICS

The siren song of the Legendary Pokémon Cards compels you to grab a deck and start dueling. But before you can master a subject, you must learn the basics. Even the Pokémon Trading Card Grand Masters began their careers as inexperienced players. This section will be your guide to the rules of the game, strategies and deck building.

IT'S IN THE CARDS

This game is a role-playing adventure based on the Pokémon Trading Card Game by Wizards of the Coast. Like the original Pokémon game, there is a story to follow and obstacles to overcome, but the main objective here is to collect and win electronic trading cards by playing against various computer opponents or against human opponents via the Game Link Cable.

Collect, Trade and Play

If you're not familiar with the Pokémon Trading Card Game (Pokémon TCG), here's the scoop. It's a two-player strategy game that uses cards to stage duels between Pokémon. Each card represents a Pokémon, an action taken by a Pokémon Trainer, or the energy used by the Pokémon to launch attacks. Using 60-card decks, players take turns attacking and defending with their Pokémon. The first to defeat all the opposing Pokémon (or to fulfill other win conditions that we'll explain later) wins the game. With the actual Trading Card Game, players obtain more cards by collecting them on their own or trading with friends. In this Game Boy game, you can obtain more cards by winning duels. When you defeat any opponent in this game, you'll be awarded two or more booster packs filled with different cards. This way, you'll be able to expand your collection and use different cards to make your decks more interesting and more powerful.

From Cardboard to Computer

Electronic Trading Cards

Pokémon Trading Card

Electronic Card

This Game Boy version of the Pokémon TCG uses many of the same cards as the real card game. They may look different from their cardboard counterparts, but the electronic cards have the same powers, abilities and attributes as the real cards. Both games play exactly the same way—the only difference is that one uses cardboard and the other uses computer chips!

New Booster Packs

You're given a deck and a few extra cards at the beginning of the game, but you must win booster packs from your rivals. These booster packs are different from the real card packs, featuring different combinations of cards.

Exclusive Cards

Even better, this game features exclusive cards that you won't find in the actual card game. These cards exist in electronic form only and can't be found in any deck or booster pack in any store!

The Adventure Begins

this game, you are an up-and-coming Pokémon TCG player who ars about four extremely rare and powerful cards. The four greatest kémon TCG masters are seeking someone worthy to inherit the ds. To claim these treasures, you must first defeat challengers from ht different Pokémon TCG clubs and then defeat the masters them- selves. You can collect and trade many different cards along the way, in the game itself and by going to the Gift Center to trade with friends via the infrared ports.

rd Combat

Story Mode

You'll collect most of your cards by winning duels. Each opponent will award you different booster packs, and you can challenge most opponents again and again. Keep in mind that most cards appear in certain boosters only.

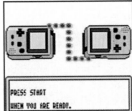

Link

To battle with a friend, connect your Game Boys with the Game Link Cable, then enter the same club's battle center. You will be able to choose how many prizes to play for.

ilding a Deck

Starter Deck

If you've already played Pokémon TCG, you can proba- bly build decks on your own. If not, you'll receive a starter deck from Dr. Mason when the game begins. You can use this deck or change it as you see fit.

Deck Machine

If you'd like help building decks, you can use the Autodeck Machines in the game. Provided you have all the proper cards, they'll build decks for you along certain strategies or themes.

ollecting More Cards

Rare Trades

Some characters in the game would rather trade than duel. If you give a collector a specif- ic card, he or she will give you another in return. The card you receive is often rare and hard to find in booster packs.

Card Pop!

You can Card Pop! with a friend if you both have a Game Boy Color and a Pokémon Trading Card Game Pak. Select Card Pop! from the menu that comes up at the start of the game, line up your infrared ports and press the A Button. You will each receive a random card. The Illusion Cards can be obtained only through Card Pop!

nformation Please

Chitchat

Many characters will want to duel or trade with you, but some simply have information you can use that might lead you to some very rare cards.

Be a Reader

Every building in the land has bookshelves filled with helpful Pokémon Trading Card Game tips. The books within each Club con- tain information about the Club's favored Pokémon type, while Dr. Mason's books give more gener- al information.

START FROM SCRATCH

This section will show you how to play the Pokémon Trading Card Game, starting with a review of the different types of cards and a look at the play area. When you begin the game, the computer will explain all of this information, but you can use this section as a reference at any time.

 ## Down to Basics

The object of the game is to knock out your opponents' Pokémon one at a time. Each of you takes turns drawing cards from your deck, playing cards from your hand and attacking or defending. Besides basic Pokémon cards, you also have Evolution 1 and 2 cards that you use to evolve your Pokémon, Energy Cards that you use to power your attacks, and Trainer Cards that allow you to take special actions. You win in any of these situations: if you knock out six of your opponent's Pokémon, if your opponent has no Pokémon left in play, or if your opponent's deck has no cards at the beginning of his or her turn. The screen shot below shows how to read a Pokémon card while the illustration on the right shows a diagram of the play area.

Pokémon Cards

Basic Pokémon Cards
These are the lowest-level Pokémon, with relatively weak attacks and low hit point levels. Hit points (HP) are used to measure a Pokémon's health.

Evolution Cards
Use Evolution cards to evolve Pokémon and make them stronger. Place Evolution 1 cards on basic Pokémon and Evolution 2 cards on Pokémon that have already evolved once. Not all Pokémon can evolve.

Energy Cards

There are seven types of energy, and each Pokémon uses a specific type or types to power its attacks. The number and type of energy needed is listed next to each attack.

Energy Types

While most Energy Cards count for one point of energy each, the Double Colorless Energy Cards are worth two points each. In addition, if an attack calls for Double Colorless Energy, you can use any type of energy to power it. For example, if an attack has two Double Colorless Energy symbols next to it, you can use one Double Colorless Energy Card or two Energy Cards of any other type to power it.

Trainer Cards

Trainer Cards allow you to take special actions not normally allowed, like drawing two cards at the beginning of your turn instead of one. These cards are used once then discarded from play.

Pokémon Card Information

Attack Cost ●
You must place Energy Cards on a Pokémon before it can attack. This shows the number and type of energy cards needed.

● Evolution
This shows if it is a basic or evolved Pokémon. A basic Pokémon cannot be evolved in the same turn it is played.

● Name

● Level/HP

● Type

● Booster
Each booster pack has a specific ID symbol. This shows which type of booster may contain this card.

Retreat ●
You can pull wounded Pokémon out of battle. This shows the energy you must discard, if any, to retreat.

● Rarity
Some cards are common and easily found, some are not. A dot means it's a common card, a diamond means it's less common, and a star means it's rare.

Weakness ●
& Resistance
Each Pokémon belongs to a different type, like Fire or Water. Any weakness to a specific type is shown here. Weakness means you take more damage than usual from that type of Pokémon; resistance means you take less.

● ID #

● Damage
This shows the amount of damage an attack causes. It is subtracted from the target's HP.

The Play Area

In the card game, the players set up an area in which to play, with certain spaces designated for certain things. This game takes place entirely within your Game Boy, of course, but the main play screens have been designed to look like a real card duel. You can switch among several different screens during a duel, allowing you to look at the overall play area, just one player's area, the cards in your hand and so on. You can look at just about everything except the cards in your opponent's hand.

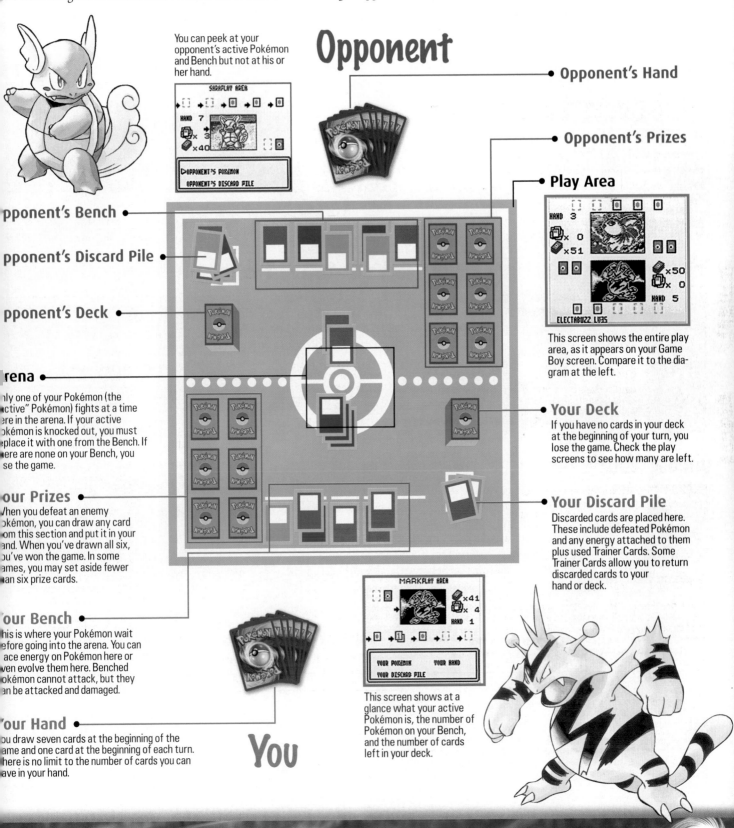

You can peek at your opponent's active Pokémon and Bench but not at his or her hand.

SEE PLAY AREA

OPPONENT'S POKéMON
OPPONENT'S DISCARD PILE

Opponent

Opponent's Hand

Opponent's Prizes

Play Area

ELECTABUZZ LV35

This screen shows the entire play area, as it appears on your Game Boy screen. Compare it to the diagram at the left.

Opponent's Bench

Opponent's Discard Pile

Opponent's Deck

Arena
Only one of your Pokémon (the "active" Pokémon) fights at a time here in the arena. If your active Pokémon is knocked out, you must replace it with one from the Bench. If there are none on your Bench, you lose the game.

Your Prizes
When you defeat an enemy Pokémon, you can draw any card from this section and put it in your hand. When you've drawn all six, you've won the game. In some games, you may set aside fewer than six prize cards.

Your Bench
This is where your Pokémon wait before going into the arena. You can place energy on Pokémon here or even evolve them here. Benched Pokémon cannot attack, but they can be attacked and damaged.

Your Hand
You draw seven cards at the beginning of the game and one card at the beginning of each turn. There is no limit to the number of cards you can have in your hand.

You

Your Deck
If you have no cards in your deck at the beginning of your turn, you lose the game. Check the play screens to see how many are left.

Your Discard Pile
Discarded cards are placed here. These include defeated Pokémon and any energy attached to them plus used Trainer Cards. Some Trainer Cards allow you to return discarded cards to your hand or deck.

MARK PLAY AREA

HAND 1

YOUR POKéMON   YOUR HAND
YOUR DISCARD PILE

This screen shows at a glance what your active Pokémon is, the number of Pokémon on your Bench, and the number of cards left in your deck.

One Step at a Time

Shuffle Your Deck

Now we'll take you through the basic steps of the game. Some of the actions described here, like shuffling the deck or dealing cards, are performed automatically by the computer. We'll describe them in detail, just so you'll know exactly what's going on at each stage of the game. Start by preparing a 60-card deck then shuffling it thoroughly.

Draw 7 Cards

Next, draw seven cards for your starting hand. If there are no basic Pokémon in your hand, put the cards back into the deck, reshuffle and draw again.

Choose Your Active Pokémon

Now select a basic Pokémon and place it on the circle in the center of the play area. This is the only time you're allowed to place a Pokémon into the arena straight from your hand. There are lots of things to consider when choosing, including whether you have the right energy in your hand to power your Pokémon.

Choose Your Bench

The next step is to choose the basic Pokémon from your hand and place them here on your Bench. You can have up to five Pokémon on your Bench at a time. You don't have to place any Pokémon here at this point, but keep in mind that if your active Pokémon is knocked out on the first turn and you have nothing on your Bench, you will lose immediately.

Coin Toss

Once your Bench is set, toss a coin to see who goes first. If you receive a heads, you go first; if it's tails, your opponent takes the first turn.

Place Prize Cards

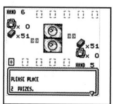

You'll then draw prize cards from your deck and place them in the prize area. Depending on what your opponent may want, you may place two, three, four or six cards there. When you knock out an opposing Pokémon, you can pick up any one of these cards.

Play Area

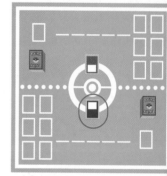

Active Pokémon

Your Bench

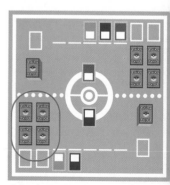

Prize Area

Turnabout Is Fair Play

When all active and Benched Pokémon are ready for action, the person who won the toss begins his or her turn. Drawing a card from the deck is always the first thing you do. Once you attack, your turn ends automatically, so save that for last. Any other actions, like those shown in the box below, can be done in any order.

Draw a Card

The first thing you do is take a card from your deck and put it in your hand. There's no limit to the number of cards you can have in your hand, but if there are no cards left in your deck, you lose the duel.

Bench a Basic Pokémon

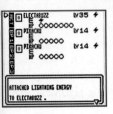

As we said, you can take almost any action in any order, but it's a good idea to place any basic Pokémon from your hand on the Bench after you draw. You cannot evolve a Pokémon that is still in your hand, and a basic Pokémon must be on the Bench for at least one turn before you evolve it.

Evolve a Pokémon

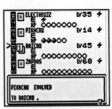

Evolution Cards are used to evolve Pokémon already in play and cannot be used on their own. An Evolution 1 card must be placed on its matching basic card, and an Evolution 2 card must be placed on its matching Evolution 1 card. A Pokémon can be evolved only once per turn, no matter how long it has been in play.

Attach an Energy Card

You can put one Energy Card into play per turn. You can attach this card to any of the Pokémon in play, either in the arena or on the Bench. Remember to refer to your Pokémon Cards to see which kind of energy they can use. Placing a Fire Energy Card on an Electric-type creature may do you little good.

Use a Pokémon Power

Some Pokémon have special abilities that are separate from their attacks and require no energy to use. These are called Pokémon Powers and can be used at any time before attacking. Complete instructions for each Pokémon Power is provided on its Pokémon's Card. Be sure to read the instructions thoroughly before using!

Play a Trainer Card

Trainer Cards allow you to perform special actions. A Trainer Card is usually used once then discarded from play. You can use as many of them in a turn as you like, and you don't have to use them all at once. If you want to use one at the beginning of your turn and one just before your attack, that's fine.

Retreat Your Active Pokémon

If your active Pokémon is wounded and you don't want it to be knocked out, you can pull it back to the Bench. In most cases, you must discard one or more Energy Cards attached to the Pokémon to pull it out. A Pokémon cannot retreat if there is no Pokémon on the Bench to take its place in the arena.

ATTACK!

This is the last action in any turn. You must have the correct type and amount of energy attached to your Pokémon to launch an attack. When the attack is resolved, your opponent's turn will begin automatically.

Damage Order

There are seven factors that can affect the outcome of a battle, and each factor is calculated separately and in a particular order. The first factor is the base damage rating for the attack. The second is any ability a Pokémon may have that affects combat. For example, if you use Scyther's Sword Dance on one turn, its Slash attack will be worth double its normal power the next. The third factor is weakness and the fourth is resistance, both of which are explained below. The fifth factor is any Trainer Card that the attacking player used to affect combat, such as PlusPower. The sixth factor is any Trainer Card that the defending player used to affect combat, like Defender. The seventh and last factor to think about is any ability the defending Pokémon has that affects combat, such as Onix's Harden.

1. Base Damage — Here's an example. Let's say Scyther is attacking Cubone with Slash. The base damage is 30 points.

2. Attack Modifier — Scyther used Sword Dance the previous turn, so Slash is now worth 60 points of damage.

3. Weakness — Cubone has a weakness toward Grass-type Pokémon, which doubles the attack to 120 points.

4. Resistance — Cubone has no resistance to Grass-type Pokémon, so the attack remains the same.

5. Trainer Card/Attack — The attacking player has a PlusPower card, which adds 1[...] points, for a total of 130 points.

6. Trainer Card/Defense — The defender used Defender on Cubone on his or her previous turn, reducing the attack by 20 points.

7. Defense Modifier — The defender also used Cubone's Snivel ability last turn, reducing the attack by another 20 points.

TOTAL DAMAGE — The total attack damage comes to 90 points, which knoc[...] out Cubone. It's overkill in this case, but you get the pictu[...]

Weakness and Resistance

Just as there are different types of energy, there are also different types of Pokémon, including several subsets. Many Pokémon have a weakness or a resistance to another type. Having a weakness means that damage from that type of Pokémon is doubled. Having a resistance means that the first 30 points of damage from that type of Pokémon are canceled out. Use the arrows on the chart below to see the relationships between the types. For example, Fire-types are weak against Water-types, and Lightning-types are weak against Fighting-types. Fewer types have a natural resistance, but, for example, all Colorless-types are resistant to Psychic-types.

Energy Type	Weakness	Resistance
Psychic Pokémon	◉	—
Grass Pokémon (Grass & Bug Subset)	🔥	✊
Grass Pokémon (Poison Subset)	◉	—
Fire Pokémon	🔥	—
Water Pokémon	⚡	—
Lightning Pokémon	✊	—
Fighting Pokémon (Fighting Subset)	◉	—
Fighting Pokémon (Rock Subset)	🌿	⚡
Colorless Pokémon	✊	◉
Colorless Pokémon (Flying Subset)	⚡	✊

Battle Effects

Some attacks have special effects on their targets, such as putt[...] them to sleep or making them confused. If a Pokémon is asleep, c[...] fused or paralyzed, and another sleep, confuse or paralyze attac[...] successful, the new effect will replace the old one. A Pokémon can[...] poisoned at the same time it is asleep, confused or paralyzed, howe[...] Retreating, evolving or using a Full Heal card on a Pokémon will c[...] it of any of these conditions.

Sleep
When your Pokémon is asleep, it can't retreat or attack. After each turn, you must flip a coin. If it's heads, your Pokémon is cured. If it comes up tails, your Pokémon remains asleep.

Paralyze
Shortened to "Parlyz" in the game, t[...] paralyze effect freezes a Pokémon s[...] that it can't retreat or attack. The affected Pokémon is cured automati[...] cally after its Trainer's next turn.

Poison
If your Pokémon is poisoned, it takes 10 points of damage at the end of every turn—yours and your opponent's. A Pokémon can't be doubly poisoned; any new poison effect replaces the old one.

Confuse
If your Pokémon is confused, you mu[...] flip a coin whenever it tries to retrea[...] or attack. If you lose the toss, your Pokémon either won't retreat or wil[...] attack itself for 20 points of damage[...]

Battle Screen

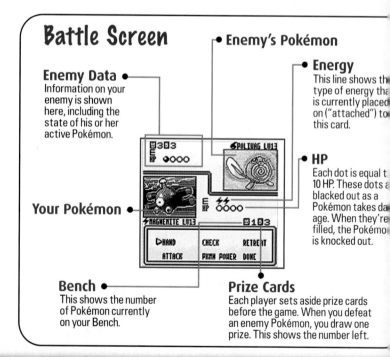

Enemy's Pokémon

Enemy Data — Information on your enemy is shown here, including the state of his or her active Pokémon.

Energy — This line shows th[...] type of energy tha[...] is currently placed[...] on ("attached") to this card.

Your Pokémon

HP — Each dot is equal t[...] 10 HP. These dots a[...] blacked out as a Pokémon takes da[...] age. When they're filled, the Pokémo[...] is knocked out.

Bench — This shows the number of Pokémon currently on your Bench.

Prize Cards — Each player sets aside prize cards before the game. When you defeat an enemy Pokémon, you draw one prize. This shows the number left.

ttack Variations

hile most combat is straightforward, it esn't always mean just doling out damage to opponent automatically. Some attacks may quire a coin toss to determine the outcome r example, heads it succeeds, tails it esn't), while others may cause effects other an damage. It pays to learn everything about ur Pokémon's abilities, because you never now when one small factor may make all the fference between a turn in the winner's circle d another round of combat. Check out the amples at the right to see many different nds of attacks and some of the side effects at can result from them.

 Poliwag Level 13 Water Gun

1. Add Energy and Stir
Add 10 points of damage to Water Gun by placing an extra Water Energy on Poliwag (in addition to the base attack cost) before attacking.

 Doduo Level 10 Fury Attack

2. Coin Toss
To calculate Fury Attack's base damage, you must flip two coins, then multiply the number of heads by 10.

 Weedle Level 12 Poison Sting

3. Combat Effects
Many attacks, like Poison Sting, can poison their targets, confuse them, paralyze them or put them to sleep.

 Chansey Level 55 Scrunch

4. Side Effects
Some attacks have side effects on later turns—Scrunch will prevent any damage to Chansey on the opponent's next turn, for example.

 Bulbasaur Level 13 Leech Seed

5. Recover HP
If Leech Seed hits for at least 10 damage, you may remove 10 damage from Bulbasaur. Many attacks have side benefits for you.

 Hitmonlee Level 30 Stretch Kick

6. Attack Bench
Attacks like Stretch Kick strike Pokémon on the Bench and not the active Pokémon. Weakness and resistance may not apply to these attacks.

Let's Rumble!

ow let's walk through a sample duel. Follow the action y reading the numbered steps and looking at the mapped lay areas and icons. This sample is mostly to illustrate he rules and flow of the game but contains general trategies, too.

Icons

 Basic Pokemon

 Grass Energy

 Psychic Energy

 Evolution 1

 Fire Energy

 Fighting Energy

 Evolution 2

 Water Energy

 Double Colorless Energy

Lightning Energy

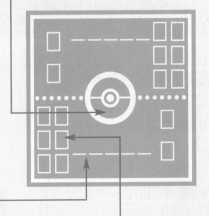

Your Pre-game Setup

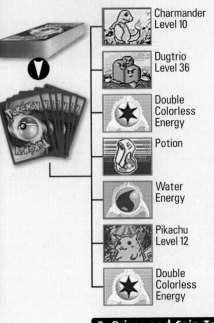

Charmander Level 10

Dugtrio Level 36

Double Colorless Energy

Potion

Water Energy

Pikachu Level 12

Double Colorless Energy

1. Choose Your Weapon!
As usual, you begin by shuffling your deck and drawing seven cards, shown at the left. You decide to use Charmander as your first active Pokémon. You take it out of your hand and place it in the arena.

2. Select Your Bench Warmers
Now you select Pikachu and place it on your Bench. Dugtrio can be used only to evolve Diglett, so it can't be used right now.

3. Prizes and Coin Toss

??? ??? ??? ???

For this game, you and your opponent agree on four prize cards, which you place in the prize area. You win the coin toss, so you go first.

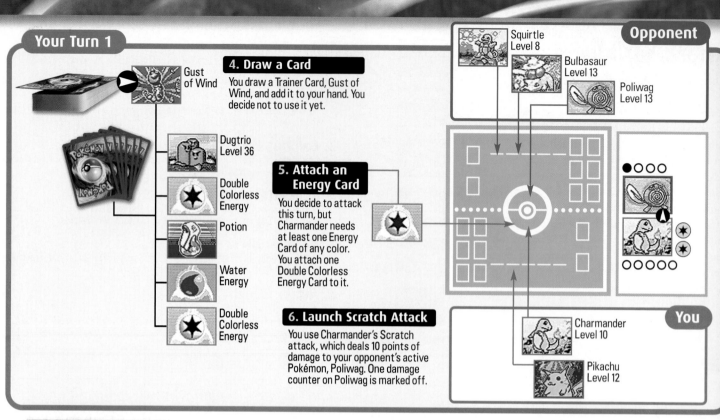

Your Turn 1

Gust of Wind

4. Draw a Card
You draw a Trainer Card, Gust of Wind, and add it to your hand. You decide not to use it yet.

Dugtrio Level 36

Double Colorless Energy

Potion

Water Energy

Double Colorless Energy

5. Attach an Energy Card
You decide to attack this turn, but Charmander needs at least one Energy Card of any color. You attach one Double Colorless Energy Card to it.

6. Launch Scratch Attack
You use Charmander's Scratch attack, which deals 10 points of damage to your opponent's active Pokémon, Poliwag. One damage counter on Poliwag is marked off.

Opponent
Squirtle Level 8
Bulbasaur Level 13
Poliwag Level 13

You
Charmander Level 10
Pikachu Level 12

Opponent's Turn 1

7. Draw a Card
Your opponent draws a card from the deck.

8. Attach an Energy Card
Your opponent attaches one Water Energy Card to Poliwag.

9. Water Gun Attack
Your opponent then uses Poliwag's Water Gun attack. This attack is normally worth 10 points of damage. Fire-type Pokémon like Charmander have a weakness against Water-types like Poliwag, though, so the damage is doubled.

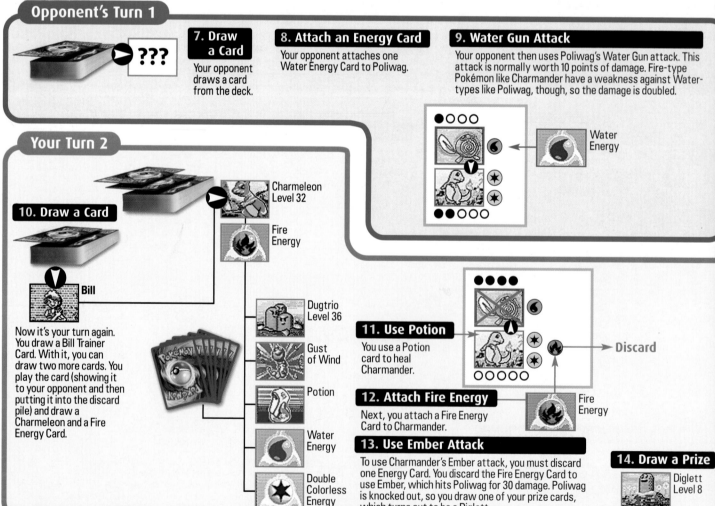

Your Turn 2

10. Draw a Card

Bill

Now it's your turn again. You draw a Bill Trainer Card. With it, you can draw two more cards. You play the card (showing it to your opponent and then putting it into the discard pile) and draw a Charmeleon and a Fire Energy Card.

Charmeleon Level 32
Fire Energy

Dugtrio Level 36
Gust of Wind
Potion
Water Energy
Double Colorless Energy

Water Energy

11. Use Potion
You use a Potion card to heal Charmander.

12. Attach Fire Energy
Next, you attach a Fire Energy Card to Charmander.

Fire Energy

Discard

13. Use Ember Attack
To use Charmander's Ember attack, you must discard one Energy Card. You discard the Fire Energy Card to use Ember, which hits Poliwag for 30 damage. Poliwag is knocked out, so you draw one of your prize cards, which turns out to be a Diglett.

14. Draw a Prize
Diglett Level 8

Opponent's Turn 2

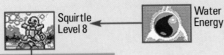

15. Choose a New Active Pokémon

With Poliwag knocked out, your opponent must select a new active Pokémon from the Bench. Squirtle's water power should be effective against Charmander.

16. Draw a card

Your opponent draws a card and surveys the play area.

Squirtle Level 8

Water Energy

17. Attach Water Energy

Your opponent attaches an Energy Card to Squirtle.

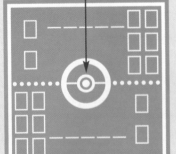

18. Use Energy Removal

Your opponent then plays an Energy Removal Card, which removes an Energy Card from one of your Pokémon and places it in your discard pile. Your opponent uses the card to remove the Double Colorless Energy Card from Charmander.

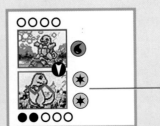

Energy Removal

Discard

19. Bubble Attack

To end the turn, your opponent launches Squirtle's Bubble attack. With Charmander's weakness, Bubble hits for 20 points. It also has a special effect, which paralyzes Charmander where it stands.

Your Turn 3

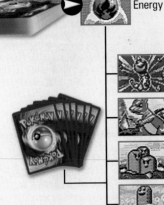

Fire Energy

Gust of Wind

Charmeleon Level 32

Dugtrio Level 36

Diglett Level 8

Water Energy

Double Colorless Energy

20. Draw a Card

You draw a Fire Energy Card and attach a Double Colorless Energy Card to Charmander. Charmander is paralyzed and can't attack, so you end your turn.

21. Play Gust of Wind

Use your Gust of Wind card to switch your opponent's active Pokémon with the Bulbasaur on the Bench. You hope that your opponent has no energy left to power Bulbasaur, leaving it helpless.

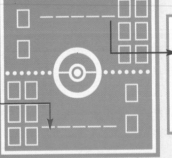

22. Place Diglett

You put Diglett onto your Bench.

23. Attach Double Colorless Energy

Attach a Double Colorless Energy Card to Charmander. Charmander is paralyzed and can't attack, so you end your turn.

 ???

24. Draw a Card

Water Energy

25. Attach Water Energy

Your opponent draws a Water Energy Card. Instead of attaching it to Bulbasaur, your opponent places it on Squirtle. The plan is to power up Squirtle, evolve it into Wartortle and then switch it back to active status. In the meantime, Bulbasaur will act as a shield.

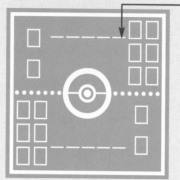

Your Turn 4

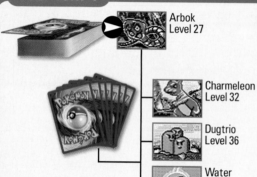

Arbok
Level 27

Charmeleon
Level 32

Dugtrio
Level 36

Water
Energy

Fire
Energy

26. Draw a Card

You draw an Arbok, which is no help in this situation.

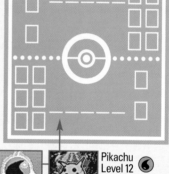

27. Attach Water Energy

Moving on, you attach a Water Energy Card to Pikachu.

  Pikachu Level 12

28. Scratch Attack

The paralyze effect fades after one turn, so Charmander is free to attack. Bulbasaur is weak against Fire-types, so Charmander's Scratch hits it for 20 points.

Opponent's Turn 4

???

29. Draw a Card

You've probably been able to glean a few general tips from the duel so far. For example, it's sometimes better to neglect an active Pokémon in favor of one on the Bench in order to produce a more powerful, evolved creature.

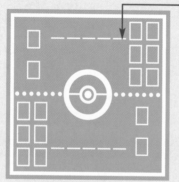

30. Evolve Squirtle

After drawing a card, your opponent evolves Squirtle by placing an Evolution 1 Wartortle card on it. Neglecting Bulbasaur again in favor of the much more powerful Wartortle, your opponent attaches an Energy Card to Wartortle and ends the turn.

 Water Energy

31. Attach Water Energy

It's also a good idea to place extra energy on a Pokémon before you evolve it, so that it will have enough energy to attack as soon as it changes.

Your Turn 5

 Fire Energy

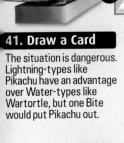

Charmeleon Level 32

Dugtrio Level 36

Fire Energy

Arbok Level 27

32. Draw a Card

This time around, you draw a Fire Energy Card.

33. Attach Fire Energy to Diglett

You attach the Fire Energy Card to Diglett. It doesn't use Fire Energy, but its evolved counterpart, Dugtrio, can use some energy of any color.

34. Scratch Attack

You attack Bulbasaur with Scratch, which hits for 20 damage and knocks it out.

35. Draw a Prize

You pick up one of your prize cards, which turns out to be a PlusPower Trainer Card.

 PlusPower

Opponent's Turn 5

 ???

Watortle Level 22

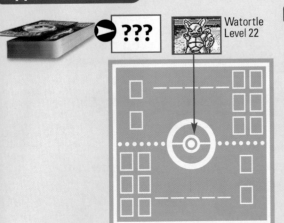

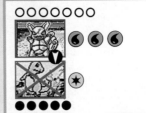

36. Play Wartortle

Wartortle was chosen to take Bulbasaur's place in the arena.

37. Draw a Card

38. Attack

Your enemy leaps to the attack with Wartortle's Bite, which takes a big enough chunk out of Charmander's HP to knock it out.

???

39. Draw a Prize

Your triumphant foe picks up a prize card.

Your Turn 6

 Lightning Energy

41. Draw a Card

The situation is dangerous. Lightning-types like Pikachu have an advantage over Water-types like Wartortle, but one Bite would put Pikachu out.

40. Play Pikachu

Pikachu Level 12

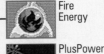

Charmeleon Level 32

Dugtrio Level 36

Fire Energy

PlusPower

Arbok Level 27

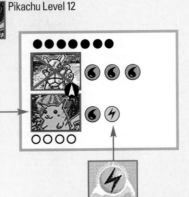

42. Attach Lightning Energy

You draw a Lightning Energy Card and attach it to Pikachu.

43. Play PlusPower

You then play your PlusPower card, which adds 10 points to any attack.

44. Thunder Jolt Attack

You launch Pikachu's Thunder Jolt, which hits for twice its normal 30 points. With the extra 10 points from the PlusPower, you hit Wartortle for a total of 70 points, knocking it out. Your astonished foe has no Pokémon on the Bench to act as a replacement, so you are declared the winner!

ADVANCED COMBAT

By now, you have a good idea of how the Pokémon Trading Card Game works. There are oth[er] factors, however, that can affect combat. While the game will calculate combat results [for] you, you should know how the entire system works, so you won't be taken by surprise wh[en] an attack you thought would knock out a foe ends up barely scratching it.

 ## Pokémon Power List

Some Pokémon have special powers besides their regular attacks. The Powers have a wide range of effects, from increasing or blocking damage to allowing players to move Energy Cards or damage counters from one creature to another. Below is a list of all the Pokémon Powers in [the] game. You cannot use a creature's Pokémon Power if it is asleep, confu[sed] or paralyzed, and you must use Pokémon Powers before you attack.

Aerodactyl Lev. 28
Prehistoric Power

This power prevents Evolution cards from being played. It stops working while Aerodactyl is asleep, confused, or paralyzed.

Alakazam Lev. 42
Damage Swap

As often as you like during your turn, you can move one damage counter from one of your Pokémon to another as long as you don't knock out that Pokémon.

Articuno Lev. 37
Quickfreeze

When you put Articuno into play during your turn (not during setup), flip a coin. If heads, the defending Pokémon will be paralyzed.

Blastoise Lev. 52
Rain Dance

As often as you like during your turn, attach one Water Energy to one of your Water-type Pokémon. This is in addition to your normal energy attachment for the turn.

Charizard Lev. 76
Energy Burn

As often as you like during your turn, you can turn all Energy attached to Charizard into Fire Energy for the rest of the turn.

Dodrio Lev. 28
Retreat Aid

As long as Dodrio is on the Bench, pay one Energy Card less (any type) to retreat your active Pokémon.

Dragonite Lev. 41
Healing Wind

When you put Dragonite into play, remove up to two damage counters from each of your Pokémon.

Dragonite Lev. 45
Step In

Once during your turn, if Dragonite is on your Bench, you may switch it with your active Pokémon.

Gengar Lev. 38
Curse

Once during your turn, you can move one damage counter from one of your opponent's Pokémon to another, even if it would knock out the other Pokémon.

Haunter Lev. 17
Transparency

Whenever an attack does anything to Haunter, flip a coin. If heads, prevent all damage and effects done to Haunter.

Kabuto Lev. 9
Kabuto Armor

Any attack that hits Kabuto does only half the damage to Kabuto rounded down to the nearest 10. Other effects still happen.

Machamp Lev. 67
Strikes Back

When an opponent's attack damages Machamp (even if Machamp is knocked out), 10 damage points are applied to the attacker. (Don't apply weakness and resistance to the counterattack.)

Mankey Lev. 7
Peek

Once during your turn, look at one of the following: the top card of either player's deck, any card from your opponent's hand, or one of either player's prizes.

Mew Lev. 8
Neutralizing Shield

This prevents all effects, including damage, done to Mew by evolved Pokémon (including your own). It stops working while Mew is asleep, confused or paralyzed.

Moltres Lev. 37
Firegiver

When you put Moltres into play during your turn, put from one to four (chosen at random) Fire Energy Cards from your deck into your hand then shuffle.

Mr. Mime Lev. 28
Invisible Wall

When an attack (even your own) does a total of 30 or more damage to Mr. Mime, prevent that damage. Any other effects still happen.

Muk Lev. 34
Toxic Gas

Ignore all Pokémon Powers other than Toxic Gases. This power stops working while Muk is asleep, confused or paralyzed.

Omanyte Lev. 19
Clairvoyance

Your opponent plays with his or her hand face up. This power stops working while Omanyte is asleep, confused, or paralyzed.

Slowbro Lev. 26
Strange Behavior

As often as you like during your turn, move one damage counter from one of your Pokémon to Slowbro as long as you don't knock out Slowbro.

Snorlax Lev. 20
Thick-Skinned

With this power, Snorlax can't be confused, paralyzed, put to sleep or poisoned. It can't be used if Snorlax is already confused, paralyzed or asleep.

Tentacool Lev. 10
Cowardice

Except on the turn Tentacool is put into play, you can return Tentacool to your hand. Discard all cards attached to Tentacool.

Venomoth Lev. 28
Shift

Once a turn, you can change Venomo[th's] type to that of any Pokémon in play other than a Colorless.

Venusaur Lev. 64
Solar Power

Use this before your attack. Your act[ive] and the defending Pokémon will no longer be asleep, confused, paralyze[d] or poisoned. It can't be used if Venus[aur] is asleep, confused or paralyzed.

Venusaur Lev. 67
Energy Trans

As often as you like during your turn, you can move one Grass Energy from one of your Pokémon to another.

Vileplume Lev. 35
Heal

Once during your turn, you may flip a co[in. If] the coin comes up heads, remove one da[m]age counter from one of your Pokémon.

Zapdos Lev. 68
Peal of Thunder

When you put Zapdos into play durin[g] your turn, do 30 damage to a Pokémo[n] other than Zapdos chosen at random. (Don't apply weakness and resistanc[e.])

Card Combos

s often possible to combine two attacks, abilities or Trainer Cards to eate a devastating attack or a beneficial effect for the attacking ayer. We've provided some examples of card combos below, and we ncourage you to create some of your own.

Energy Crisis

 Venusaur
Level 67
Energy Trans
+
 Charizard
Level 76
Energy Burn

Health Insurance

 Venusaur
Level 67
Energy Trans
+
 Pokémon Center

Clean Sweep

 Venusaur
Level 67
Energy Trans
+
 Mr. Fuji

Clean Sweep II

 Alakazam
Level 42
Damage Swap
+
 Tentacool
Level 10
Cowardice

Temper Tantrum

 Alakazam
Level 42
Damage Swap
+
 Dodrio
Level 28
Rage

Stormy Weather

 Pokémon Flute
+
 Gust of Wind

Energy Overload

 Venusaur
Level 67
Energy Trans
+
 Exeggutor
Level 35
Big Eggsplosion

Energy Recycle

 Mewtwo
Level 60
Energy Absorption
+
 Mr. Fuji

Let's say you'd like to use Charizard's Fire Spin attack, but you're two Fire Energy Cards short. First use Venusaur's Energy Trans power to move two Grass Energy Cards to Charizard. Now use Charizard's Energy Burn power to change the Grass Energy into Fire Energy. No more energy crisis!

Venusaur has been wounded badly. You'd like to heal it with the Pokémon Center Card, but you don't want to pay the energy costs. What will you do? Simply use Energy Trans to move Venusaur's Grass Energy Cards to another creature before you use Pokémon Center. If Venusaur has no energy, the healing is free!

Once again, Venusaur is in trouble. It's taken a lot of damage, and you're going to use Mr. Fuji to place it back into the deck before it's knocked out. You could use Venusaur's Grass Energy right away, though, so you transfer the Energy Cards to your other Pokémon in play before whisking Venusaur away.

Clean Sweep works only for Venusaur, but if you have Alakazam and Tentacool in play, you can use Clean Sweep II to help any Pokémon in trouble. Simply use Damage Swap to transfer damage from any of your Pokémon to Tentacool, then use Cowardice to return Tentacool to your hand. No muss, no fuss!

If your Dodrio is in the arena, use Alakazam's Damage Swap to give it as much damage as it can take without being knocked out. Damage actually adds power to Dodrio's Rage attack. With this tactic, you can deliver up to 70 points of damage in one blow!

Use the Pokémon Flute card to take a Pokémon from your opponent's discard pile and place it on his or her Bench. Try to find one with a weakness to your active Pokémon. Now use Gust of Wind to switch the newly recycled Pokémon with your opponent's active creature. This should be an easy K.O.!

Here's another big combo that has the potential to wipe out even the toughest defender. Use Energy Trans to move all of Venusaur's Grass Energy to Exeggutor. With Big Eggsplosion, you flip a coin for every Energy Card on Exeggutor, then multiply the number of heads by 20. Get the picture?

Use Energy Absorption to take two Energy Cards from your discard pile and attach them to Mewtwo, and then use Mr. Fuji to return Mewtwo and any attached cards to your deck. Sneaky!

Building a Deck

By now, you're probably anxious to build your own Pokémon TCG decks. The first question many players ask is, "How many different types of energy and Pokémon should I use?" The answer is one or two, at least until you have more experience. Why? Consider that you have only 60 cards in a deck, which must be split among Pokémon, Trainer and Energy Cards. If you have three or more types of energy and Pokémon, you may not draw what you need when you need it. Two-type decks are much easier to balance, and you can be reasonably sure you won't end up with a huge energy surplus or shortage. If you do construct a three-type deck, try using a small number of Colorless Pokémon as the third type, since they can use any type of energy.

In the Beginning

 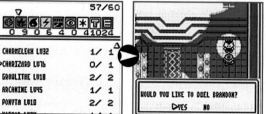

You begin the game with one deck and some extra cards. As you win duels, you'll collect booster packs of new cards. You can use these cards to modify your existing deck or build new ones. Different opponents will use different types of energy and Pokémon, so you must tailor your decks to meet each new challenge.

Basic Rules and Limits

While you can construct your decks in many different ways, there are a few rules to follow. Of course, a deck must have 60 cards. There's no limit on the total number of Energy Cards, but you're limited to four Double Colorless Energy Cards. (Remember that Double Colorless Cards count as one card but have two energy points on them.) Finally, you can use no more than four of any Pokémon Card or Trainer Card.

 Energy Card
No Limit

 Double Colorless Energy Card
Max 4

Basic Pokemon Card

Evolution Card

Trainer Card

The four-card limit on these types of cards prevents players from overloading their decks with any one thing.

Balancing Act

Now that you know what not to do, here are our recommendations for what you should do. The first thing is to find a balance between the different types of cards. You must have enough energy to power your Pokémon's attacks and enough Trainer Cards to support your Pokémon in combat. For beginning decks, we recommend using 20-26 Pokémon cards, 10-16 Trainer Cards and 24-28 Energy Cards. While 20 Pokémon may be fewer than is advisable in some situations, if you have the right Trainer Cards, you'll do fine. The next task is to balance the number of basic Pokémon to evolved Pokémon. There should always be more basic Pokémon than Evolution 1 Pokémon, and more Evolution 1 than Evolution 2. When looking at one evolutionary line, using four basic, three Evolution 1 and two Evolution 2 Pokémon is a good start. If a Pokemon has no second evolution, try four basic and two or three Evolution 1, or three basic and two Evolution 1 creatures.

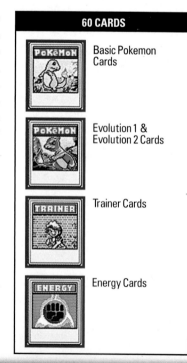

60 CARDS

Basic Pokemon Cards

Evolution 1 & Evolution 2 Cards

Trainer Cards

Energy Cards

EVOLUTION RATIO

Basic Pokémon x4

Evolution 1 x3

Evolution 2 x2

Starter Decks

When you begin the game, you'll choose from three pre-constructed starter decks. You may want to modify your deck as you gain experience, earn cards and develop a playing style.

Squirtle & Friends

We suggest using single-type decks early in the game. If you have enough Water-type cards, dump the Fighting-types and Psychic-types in favor of finny friends. Keep the Colorless-types, since energy isn't a problem for them. This deck would work well against Fire-types.

Bulbasaur & Friends

Like all the starter decks, this deck suffers from too many different cards and too many single cards. Reduce the number of evolutionary lines to just three or four. If you can, drop the Grass-types when fighting Fire-type foes, and drop the Water-types when battling Fighting/Rock foes.

Charmander & Friends

This deck emphasizes Fire-type and Lightning-type Pokémon. If you have the right cards, swap the Fighting- and Colorless-types for Fire- and Lightning types, and double up on your favorite Trainer Cards. This deck would work best against Grass-type and Water-type decks.

TYPE	NAME	LEVEL	# OF CARDS
	Charmander	10	2
	→Charmeleon	32	1
	→Charizard	76	1
	Growlithe	18	2
	→Arcanine	45	1
	Ponyta	10	2
	Magmar	24	1
	Pikachu	12	2
	→Raichu	40	1
	Magnemite	13	2
	→Magneton	28	1
	Zapdos	64	1
	Diglett	8	2
	→Dugtrio	36	1
	Machop	20	1
	→Machoke	40	1
	Rattata	9	2
	→Raticate	41	1
	Meowth	14	1

ENERGY CARDS	# OF CARDS
Fire Energy	10
Thunder Energy	8
Fighting Energy	6

TRAINER CARDS	# OF CARDS
Professor Oak	1
Bill	2
Switch	1
Computer Search	1
PlusPower	1
Potion	2
Full Heal	2

TYPE	NAME	LEVEL	# OF CARDS
	Squirtle	8	2
	→Wartortle	22	1
	→Blastoise	52	1
	Seel	12	2
	→Dewgong	42	1
	Goldeen	12	1
	→Seaking	28	1
	Staryu	15	1
	→Starmie	28	1
	Lapras	31	1
	Machop	20	1
	→Machoke	40	1
	Geodude	16	2
	Hitmonchan	33	1
	Abra	10	2
	→Kadabra	28	1
	Gastly	8	2
	→Haunter	22	1
	Rattata	9	2
	→Raticate	41	1
	Meowth	14	1

ENERGY CARDS	# OF CARDS
Water Energy	11
Fighting Energy	6
Psychic Energy	8

TRAINER CARDS	# OF CARDS
Professor Oak	1
Bill	1
Switch	1
Poké Ball	1
Scoop Up	1
Item Finder	1
Potion	1
Full Heal	1

TYPE	NAME	LEVEL	# OF CARDS
	Bulbasaur	13	2
	→Ivysaur	20	1
	→Venusaur	67	1
	Caterpie	13	2
	→Metapod	21	1
	Nidoran ♀	13	2
	Nidoran ♂	20	2
	→Nidorino	25	1
	Tangela	12	1
	Seel	12	1
	→Dewgong	42	1
	Krabby	20	2
	→Kingler	27	1
	Goldeen	12	2
	→Seaking	28	1
	Jigglypuff	14	1
	Meowth	14	1
	Kangaskhan	40	1
	Eevee	12	2
	→Flareon	28	1
	→Vaporeon	42	1

ENERGY CARDS	# OF CARDS
Grass Energy	11
Fire Energy	3
Water Energy	9

TRAINER CARDS	# OF CARDS
Professor Oak	1
Switch	1
Poké Ball	1
PlusPower	2
Defender	1
Full Heal	2
Revive	1

Deck Doctoring

Here are two examples that may help illustrate our deck-building principles and techniques. First is a deck that, while workable, has a few problems. We're going to tweak it until it's fighting trim. Once again, you don't have to build decks along our guidelines, but they are a good place to start. Once you have more experience, you can experiment on your own to find out what works best for you.

Before

In this deck, your Fire-types have much greater energy needs than your Lightning-types. When selecting energy, keep an eye on both the number of Pokémon and the energy needed for the individual attacks you intend to use.

The Fire/Lightning combination is a good one (Fire-types are weak against Water-types, but Lightning-types can trounce Water-types). However, your Pokémon are spread too thinly among too many different evolutionary lines/groups, and the ratios of basic to evolved Pokémon are off.

TYPE	NAME	LEVEL	# OF CARDS
🔥	Charmander	10	2
🔥	➤Charmeleon	32	2
🔥	Vulpix	11	2
🔥	➤Ninetales	35	2
🔥	Ponyta	10	2
🔥	➤Rapidash	33	1
🔥	Magmar	24	1
🔥	Magmar	31	1
⚡	Pikachu	12	2
⚡	➤Raichu	40	1
⚡	Voltorb	10	2
⚡	➤Electrode	42	1
⚡	Electabuzz	35	1

ENERGY CARDS	# OF CARDS
Fire Energy	8
Lightning Energy	18

TRAINER CARDS	# OF CARDS
Professor Oak	1
Bill	2
Energy Search	2
Switch	2
Poké Ball	2
PlusPower	1
Defender	1
Potion	2
Full Heal	1

Normally, we recommend havi[ng] at least two of any card in you[r] deck, at least when you're jus[t] starting out. That way, there's [a] better chance of actually draw[ing] a card when you need it. In this case, though, Professor Oak a[nd] Bill have similar functions, so h[av]ing just one Professor Oak is fi[ne].

Now here's where you should d[ou]ble up on some cards and disca[rd] others. One PlusPower or one Defender won't make much of [a] difference in the long run.

After

This deck is by no means perfect, but it's a good start. It's balanced and has the beginnings of what you'll need to execute solid battle strategy. As you proceed, just keep these basic deck-building techniques in mind. You may end up with different ratios and numbers of cards that work for you, and that's great. But if your deck just isn't working, it may help to break it down completely before you build it back up.

This selection of Pokémon should be much better. There are more creatures in the deck now, but they're better organized in just four evolutionary lines/groups, and the ratios of basic to evolved Pokémon have been fixed.

The specific Pokémon have also been chosen for specific purposes. The Magmar cards are for quick and cheap defense, the Charmander line is for big Fire attacks and the two Lightning-type groups are there to harass your opponent's Bench.

TYPE	NAME	LEVEL	# OF CARDS
🔥	Charmander	10	4
🔥	➤Charmeleon	32	3
🔥	➤Charizard	76	2
🔥	Magmar	24	2
🔥	Magmar	31	2
⚡	Pikachu	12	3
⚡	➤Raichu	45	2
⚡	Voltorb	10	3
⚡	➤Electrode	42	2

ENERGY CARDS	# OF CARDS
Fire Energy	13
Lightning Energy	13

TRAINER CARDS	# OF CARDS
Bill	3
Energy Search	2
Energy Retrieval	2
Potion	2
Full Heal	2

Your energy needs will likely ba[l]ance out. While your Lightning-type attacks are generally mor[e] expensive, you have more Fire-type Pokémon in the deck, and you'll draw them more often.

The single cards have been toss[ed] out in favor of doubling up on ba[sic] Trainer Cards, like Potion and Fu[ll] Heal. Always keep an eye out fo[r] cards that can help in almost an[y] situation, like Potion and Heal, a[s] well as cards that support specific strategies. For exampl[e,] this deck can be power hungry [at] times, so we also included two Energy Search and two Energy Retrieval Cards.

In the end, we decided to drop the lone Professor Oak in favor of three Bill cards. With this deck, you may want to keep your options open and not throw away any cards needlessly. Besides, even if you don't need a particular card anymore, it's better to use it with an Energy Retrieval than just to toss it into the discard pile.

CHALLENGE THE MASTERS

Now that you've learned the basics, you are ready to begin your quest to inherit the Legendary Pokémon Cards. If you defeat all eight Pokémon Trading Card Club Masters, you will earn the right to challenge the Grand Masters. Then the Legendary Pokémon Cards will be yours— unless your rival gets there first...

WORLD MAP

This is the wondrous land where your quest will take place. You'll begin in Mason Laboratory, on the southwest corner of the island. Where you go from there will be up to you, but all paths will lead eventually to the Pokémon Dome and a showdown with the card masters. With a bit of skill and luck, you just might claim the Legendary Pokémon Cards for yourself!

CHALLENGE HALL

ISHIHARA'S HOUSE

PSYCHIC CLUB

ROCK CLUB

POKéMON DOME

LIGHTNING CLUB

MASON LABORATORY

FIGHTING CLUB

Mason Laboratory

Dr. Mason is one of the world's foremost experts on Pokémon cards. He's graciously offered you the use of his lab whenever you want. His computers can construct decks for you or allow you to save ones you create yourself. Either way, his services will prove invaluable as you embark on your quest to win the Legendary Pokémon Cards.

Library

Dr. Mason's library is crammed with books on the Pokémon Trading Card Game. It would be good to review them before you build your first deck or fight your first duel.

Autodeck Machines

These machines can create new decks for you, provided you have the proper cards. Use the medals you win from the Club champions to activate the machines.

PC

There are PCs in the good doctor's lab and in all the Card Clubs. Use the PCs to read e-mail from Dr. Mason and receive booster packs from him.

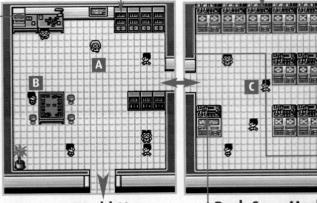

World Map

Deck Save Machine

This machine can save decks you create yourself. If you save a deck and then modify or deconstruct it, you can return here and have the machine rebuild it the way it was when you saved it.

A Dr. Mason

When you first begin the game, Dr. Mason will offer to walk you through a sample duel and then give you a choice of the three starter decks we showed you earlier. You can take different paths through the game, depending on which deck you take. We recommend taking the Charmander & Friends deck and challenging the Grass Club first, and this is the path we'll show you in this section of the book. Between bouts at the various Clubs, be sure to visit the Challenge Hall to participate in regional tournaments.

B Sam

Dr. Mason's assistant, Sam, is available for practice duels and questions at any time. He can help you understand the rules of the game as well as basic strategies. He's a great resource for you early in the game.

C Aaron

Aaron is another of Dr. Mason's lab technicians. He'll duel with you whenever you want, but you'll win only Energy Cards from him. If you're short on energy, though, he's the man to see.

FIRE CLUB

SCIENCE CLUB

GRASS CLUB

WATER CLUB

GRASS CLUB

While they're not exactly pushovers, you shouldn't have much trouble mowing down the Grass Club members, provided you have the right game plan. Use the map below to identify each of the members, and follow our deck-building and play tips to sow the seeds of your success.

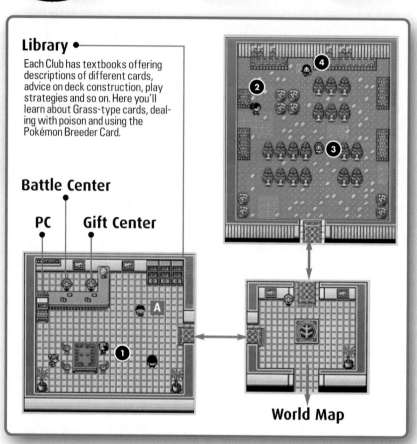

Library

Each Club has textbooks offering descriptions of different cards, advice on deck construction, play strategies and so on. Here you'll learn about Grass-type cards, dealing with poison and using the Pokémon Breeder Card.

Battle Center

PC **Gift Center**

A

1 **2** **3** **4**

World Map

A Let's Make a Deal

Some folks are more interested in trading than du[...]ing. This gal, for example, will ask you for a level[...] Oddish card. If you fork one over, she'll give yo[...] level-35 Vileplume. Later, she'll ask for a level-14 C[...]fairy and a level-76 Charizard. In return, she'll gi[...] you a special promotional Pikachu card (featuring [...] unique, level-16 creature) and a level-52 Blastoise.

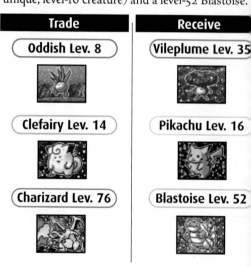

Trade	Receive
Oddish Lev. 8	Vileplume Lev. 35
Clefairy Lev. 14	Pikachu Lev. 16
Charizard Lev. 76	Blastoise Lev. 52

Your First Deck

The Charmander & Friends deck that you can build at the Mason Laboratory will work well enough, but our Fire-type deck shown at the right will give you more offensive punch. If you don't have all the cards listed or would like to try a different strategy, feel free to experiment. To point you in the right direction, we'll provide you with general descriptions of your opponents' strategies and show some of the cards they use. In addition, if an opposing Pokémon has a weakness to a particular type, we'll show the appropriate icon next to the creature's name and level number.

POKéMON CARDS	LEVEL	# OF CARDS
Charmander	10	3
► Charmeleon	32	2
Vulpix	11	3
► Ninetales	35	2
Ponyta	10	3
► Rapidash	33	2
Magmar	24	2
Magmar	31	2
Rattata	9	2

TRAINER CARDS	# OF CARDS
Bill	2
Energy Search	3
Energy Removal	2
Gust of Wind	2
Potion	2
Full Heal	2

Energy Cards	# OF CARDS
Fire Energy	22
Double Colorless Energy	4

❶ Brittany Etc. Deck
Prize Cards: 4
Win: 2 Mystery Boosters

This is your first "real" duel, so be wary. Besides using Grass-types, Brittany also likes to use Psychic-types like Gastly and Jynx to put opponents to sleep while she beefs up her Pokémon. Don't be surprised if she fields a few Lightning-type Pokémon as well, including a certain lightning-tailed creature we all know and love. Check the list to the right to see other cards she's likely to use.

Nidoran ♀ Lev. 13
Using Nidoran ♀'s Call for Family, Brittany can pull one Nidoran ♀ card from her deck and place it on her Bench. Call requires two Grass Energy Cards, so use Energy Removal to nip this danger in the bud.

Energy Search
While your Pokémon sleep peacefully under her spells, Brittany will use these cards to pull Energy Cards from her deck and place them in her hand. You may be in for a rude awakening!

Poké Ball
Poké Ball allows the player to pull any Pokémon from his or her deck and place it on the Bench. Between Call for Family and Poké Ball, Brittany is almost never caught short of Pokémon.

❷ Kristin Flower Garden Deck
Prize Cards: 4
Win: 2 Evolution Boosters

Like Brittany, Kristin favors Pokémon with paralyzing powers, like Oddish and Lickitung. As long as your Pokémon can avoid these effects, however, you should do well enough. A blow from even a basic Fire-type can take out Oddish, while a single strike from a Stage-1 or Stage-2 Fire-type will give Lickitung a pizza burn it will never forget! Just save your Full Heal Cards for crucial situations.

Oddish Lev. 8
Rapidash's Agility ability can block the effects of Oddish's Stun Spore and other paralyzing attacks for one turn. You'll have to flip a coin to see if it will work, but it won't hurt to try.

Ivysaur Lev. 20
If Kristin has the time and energy, she'll evolve at least one Bulbasaur into an Ivysaur. Your only hope against its Poison Powder attack will be to strike early or keep a Full Heal Card handy.

Lickitung Lev. 26
Lickitung can stick it to your Pokémon two ways: with a paralyzing Tongue Wrap and with a confusion-causing Supersonic. Fortunately, Tongue Wrap causes only 10 damage, but Supersonic causes none.

❸ Heather Kaleidoscope Deck
Prize Cards: 4
Win: 2 Colosseum Boosters

Heather uses a relatively small number of Grass-types. Her favorite Pokémon seems to be Eevee. Try to take it out as soon as it appears, because if it evolves into Flareon, Vaporeon or Jolteon, it will make short work of your basic Pokémon. If you have energy to spare, charge up a level-24 Magmar and keep it ready. If Eevee pops up, put Magmar in play immediately and launch a Flamethrower attack.

Porygon Lev. 12
With its Conversion power, Porygon can change its resistance and block attacks from your active Pokémon's type. Switch to a different type and attack before Porygon can convert itself again.

Ditto Lev. 19
As its name implies, Ditto can mimic the powers of any opposing Pokémon, treating the Energy Cards attached to it as energy of any type. Like the real thing, however, it can't evolve.

Eevee Lev. 12
Grass Club members delight in delaying tactics, and Eevee fits right in with that strategy. If a coin toss is successful, Eevee's Tail Wag will prevent its opponent from even launching an attack.

Club Master
❹ Nikki Flower Power Deck
Prize Cards: 6
Win: 2 Laboratory Boosters
Grass Medal
(For Grass Medal Autodeck Machine)

Unlike her peers, Nikki is a true champion of Grass-type cards. This is ironic, since it makes her particularly vulnerable to your Fire-type cards, and thus, easier to defeat than her fellow club members. Big problems will occur only if you don't evolve your Pokémon quickly enough or if you're energy poor. Otherwise, Nikki and her Pokémon will be toast in very short order!

Exeggutor Lev. 35
Nikki will try to evolve Exeggcute into Exeggutor on the Bench if possible. With 80 HP, it may be able to get in two or three Big Eggsplosions before you fry it.

Venusaur Lev. 67
With Venusaur's special Pokémon Power, Nikki can take an Energy Card from one creature and place it on another to power emergency attacks or save energy from a weakened Pokémon.

Vileplume Lev. 35
Nikki will often resort to Vileplume's Petal Dance attack. Even though it throws Vileplume into a state of confusion, it can inflict up to 120 points of damage—well worth the risk!

Pokémon Breeder
This card allows the player to place a Stage 2 evolution card directly on top of its matching basic Pokémon—a time saver for Nikki and big trouble for you.

FIRE CLUB

The tables are turned as you face Fire-type Pokémon in card combat. The Fire Club members may seem like hotheads at first, but when it comes to dueling, they're cool contenders. They load their Benches early, so pay attention to what's on the table to avoid surprises.

Library

Browse the Fire Club library for general information on Fire-type cards, advice on building and combating Fire-type decks, and some interesting tidbits about exclusive cards found only in this Game Boy game.

Battle Center

PC   **Gift Center**

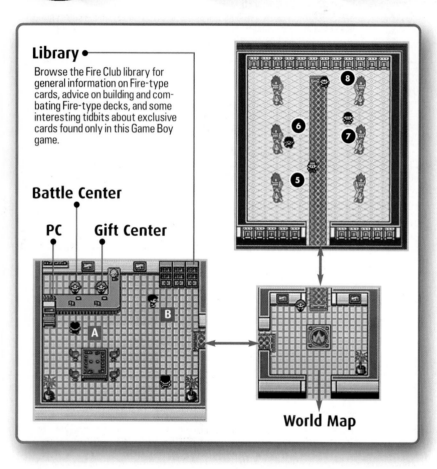

World Map

A Ishihara

Speak to this fellow to learn about Ishihara, one of the foremost Pokémon card collectors in the world. To find Ishihara, go to the house in the northwest corner of the world map. Besides a huge card collection, he also has an impressive library.

B Secret Slowpoke

Once you collect a certain number of Energy Cards, this boy will tell you how to find a hidden Slowpoke card in exchange for all the Energy Cards you're not currently using in a deck. If you refuse, he'll leave in a huff, never to return. When he demands your card, reset your game and then construct several temporary decks until you have just one Energy Card left over. Then the Slowpoke will cost you just one card.

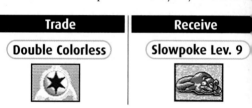

Trade	Receive
Double Colorless	Slowpoke Lev. 9

Fire Prevention

This deck relies on more than just the natural advantage that Water-type Pokémon have over Fire-type Pokémon. Many of the stronger Fire-type attacks require the attacker to discard one or more Energy Cards. The player must then replace the energy before using that attack again. With Golduck, Poliwrath and Dragonair on your side, you'll be able to rob your opponents of precious energy and, as a result, much of their offensive strength as well. Horsea and Seadra can blunt your opponents' attacks even further, provided you have a few lucky coin tosses.

POKéMON CARDS	LEVEL	# OF CARDS
Psyduck	15	3
► Golduck	27	2
Poliwag	13	3
► Poliwhirl	28	2
► Poliwrath	48	2
Horsea	19	3
► Seadra	23	2
Dratini	10	3
► Dragonair	33	2

TRAINER CARDS	# OF CARDS
Bill	2
Energy Search	2
Energy Removal	2
Gust of Wind	2
Potion	2
Full Heal	2

Energy Cards	# OF CARDS
Water Energy	22
Double Colorless Energy	4

5 John — Anger Deck

Prize Cards: 4
Win: 2 Evolution Boosters

John calls this his "Anger Deck," and rightly so. Many of his Pokémon, including Dodrio, Tauros and Cubone, become even more ferocious when wounded. Luckily, the energy-robbing strategies that you'll be using against the Fire-type Pokémon can also be effective against these irate interlopers. Our advice is to strike hard, strike fast, and not allow them to build up any energy.

 Tauros Lev. 32
Tauros's Rampage attack does 20 points of damage plus 10 more for every damage counter on Tauros. Using this ability, however, may make Tauros confused and give you a chance to respond.

 Raticate Lev. 41
Raticate may not look like much of a threat, but don't underestimate it. When it uses Super Fang, half of the defender's remaining HP is added to Raticate's attack. You do the math!

 Cubone Lev. 13
Like Tauros, Cubone can turn its own damage into extra attack power. With only 40 HP of its own, though, you'll have a good chance of taking it down in one turn.

 6 Adam — Flamethrower Deck

Prize Cards: 4
Win: 2 Colosseum Boosters

Adam doesn't use any complex strategies, but with the number of heavy hitters in his deck, he won't need any. Just focus on evolving and powering up your Pokémon as quickly as possible and keep an eye on where Adam is placing his Energy Cards. If you see him piling Energy Cards on a Benched Eevee, you can bet that he has a Flareon card in his hand, ready to go.

 Vulpix Lev. 11
Vulpix's Confuse Ray will be a source of seemingly endless frustration for you. Adam will often open with a Vulpix to give himself time to evolve an Eevee into a Flareon or power up a Magmar.

 Eevee Lev. 12
Adam can buy himself even more time with Eevee's Tail Wag ability, which can block an opponent's attack on the next turn. Adam must win a coin toss for this effect to work.

 Magmar Lev. 24
Both Flareon and Magmar have devastating Flamethrower attacks, but Magmar's is cheaper and nearly as powerful. At 50 points of damage, this attack is worth the one Energy Card you must discard.

 7 Jonathan — Reshuffle Deck

Prize Cards: 4
Win: 2 Colosseum Boosters

Like several of the players you've dueled before, Jonathan will try to hold you off with Pokémon like Jigglypuff and Wigglytuff while he prepares his big guns for battle. A Gust of Wind will put a damper on that strategy by bringing one of his Benched Pokémon (preferably one without Energy Cards attached) into the arena. Turnabout is fair play, of course, and he may try to do the same to you.

 Pidgeotto Lev. 36
Pidgeotto's Whirlwind attack works like the Gust of Wind card, except that the defending player is allowed to choose which of his or her Benched Pokémon will be placed in the arena.

 Ninetales Lev. 35
This level 35 Ninetales is head and shoulders above its predecessor, Vulpix. Its Dancing Embers attack is expensive, but it can defeat many basic Pokémon with just one blow.

Switch
Jonathan seems to use Switch Cards more than most players, forcing you to keep an eye on his bench at all times. He may use it to save a wounded Jigglypuff or spring a Ninetales on you.

 **Club Master**

8 Ken — Fire Charge Deck

Prize Cards: 6
Win: 2 Mystery Boosters
Fire Medal

(For Fire Medal Autodeck Machine)

Despite his status as the Fire Club champ, Ken doesn't always use a lot of Fire-type cards, employing a wide variety of creatures instead. Once again, the club champ may prove much easier to defeat than the lower-ranked members. In any case, you're the perfect person to fan the flames of competition and force Ken to put his money where his mouth is.

 Arcanine Lev. 45
Arcanine is one of the few Fire-types that Ken will use on a regular basis. This Pokémon that worked so well for you in your earlier duels will be turned against you!

 Jigglypuff Lev. 12
This intriguing card isn't very powerful, but it is rare. If you'd like the chance to collect one, look for a fellow named Ronald in the club lobby after you defeat Ken.

Chansey Lev. 55
Chansey's Scrunch power is not quite as effective as Horsea's Smokescreen ability. While it cancels out damage, it can't cancel out special effects like sleep, poison and so on.

 Tauros Lev. 32
As you probably realize by now, you should defeat Tauros in one turn if possible, or else it might use its own wounds to increase the power of its counterattack.

WATER CLUB

The Water Club is the next stop on your road to Pokémon stardom. If the Water Clubbers think they're going to drown your hopes of claiming the Legendary Cards, they're in for a mighty big shock, courtesy of Pikachu and a few of its high-voltage friends.

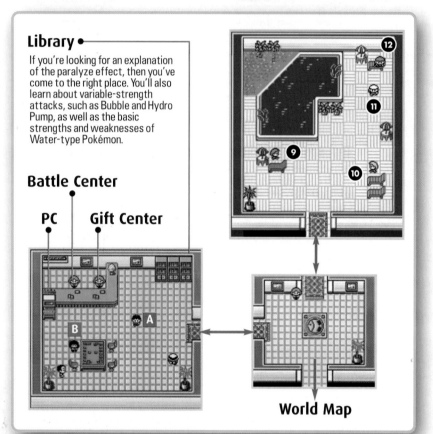

Library

If you're looking for an explanation of the paralyze effect, then you've come to the right place. You'll also learn about variable-strength attacks, such as Bubble and Hydro Pump, as well as the basic strengths and weaknesses of Water-type Pokémon.

Battle Center

PC   Gift Center

World Map

A Crazy Like a Fox

This boy will tell you about an eccentric fellow nam[ed] Imakuni?, who wanders among the various clu[bs.] After you've won a few medals, he may appear in o[ne] of the club lounges. Imakuni? may look wild and a[ct] strangely, but he's carrying a lot of booster packs.

B Fire for Water

Here's another opportunity to add to your grow[ing] collection. If you have a level-31 Lapras, this you[ng]ster will give you a level-34 Arcanine in exchang[e.] This promotional card isn't as powerful as t[he] common card, but its still-formidable attacks u[se] less energy.

Trade	Receive
Lapras Lev. 31	Arcanine Lev. 34

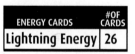

Shock Treatment

Most of the time, Pokémon can't be harmed while they're on the Bench. With the Pokémon we've picked out for this deck, however, you'll be able to reach around your opponent's active creature and strike the ones waiting on the sidelines. Because there are fewer prize cards than normal in these duels, we're adjusting some of the usual card ratios to make room for Poké Ball cards. These will help you find the evolution cards you need to evolve your Pokémon quickly.

POKÉMON CARDS	LEVEL	#OF CARDS
Pikachu	14	4
➤ Raichu	45	3
Magnemite	13	3
➤ Magneton	28	2
Electabuzz	35	3
Eevee	12	3
➤ Jolteon	24	2

TRAINER CARDS	#OF CARDS
Bill	2
Energy Retrieval	2
Energy Search	2
Energy Removal	2
Poké Ball	2
Gust of Wind	2
Potion	1
Full Heal	1

ENERGY CARDS	#OF CARDS
Lightning Energy	26

9 Sara — Waterfront Deck

Prize Cards: 2
Win: 2 Colosseum Boosters

In an unusual twist, Sara will ask that you each set aside only two prize cards. This means the game will progress very quickly, and you'll have to strike fast and strike hard. Using Self Destruct may seem risky in a two-prize game, but if none of your Pokémon has been defeated yet and the explosion would take out Sara's active Pokémon, then use it. Just make sure you have another defender ready to go.

Squirtle Lev. 8
Squirtle can block damage to itself with its Withdraw ability, but it can't do anything about attacks on its Benched brethren. If it uses Withdraw, just ignore it and target the Bench on the next turn.

Dratini Lev. 10
Dratini itself is not much of a threat, but if it evolves into Dragonair, its more cunning descendant can force you to discard Energy Cards. The remedy for that would be an Energy Retrieval card.

Slowpoke Lev. 18
Slowpoke has special abilities that spell trouble in a short game: the power to heal damage and the power to retrieve Trainer Cards from the discard pile. Don't give it a chance to use either!

10 Amanda — Lonely Friends Deck

Prize Cards: 3
Win: 2 Mystery Boosters

Many of Amanda's Pokémon are not particularly vulnerable to Lightning-types, so you may wish to swap out a few for Fire-types or Fighting-types. Otherwise, Raichu is your best bet for this duel, since it can damage up to three Benched Pokémon at a time. Besides using Scyther and Wigglytuff, Amanda will occasionally play a Mysterious Fossil and evolve it into an Omanyte.

Scyther Lev. 25
If you see Scyther use its Swords Dance ability, be ready to be rocked. Swords Dance increases its Slash attack from a base of 30 damage points to a whopping 60 damage points on the next turn.

Wigglytuff Lev. 36
Amanda will try to use your own battle strategy against you with this level-36 Wigglytuff, which can hit all of your Pokémon, active and Benched, for 10 damage points each.

Potion
Amanda packs a lot of basic Potion cards in her deck, so it's important to evolve your Pikachu into Raichu as quickly as possible. She may fend off one Gigashock attack, but not two or three.

11 Joshua — Sound of the Waves Deck

Prize Cards: 4
Win: 2 Mystery Boosters

This duel will bring you back up to the normal number of prize cards, but that doesn't mean you'll be able to take it easy. Joshua fields a lot of basic Pokémon quickly, and you'll have to do the same to keep up with him. Luckily for you, he often seems to have trouble powering up his Pokémon, and an extra Energy Removal card or two in your deck could certainly complicate matters for him even more.

Lapras Lev. 31
Joshua likes to lead off with a Lapras if he can. Lapras doesn't have much attack power, but with 80 HP and the ability to confuse its opponent, it can keep enemies at bay for a long time.

Shellder Lev. 8
Though it can confuse opponents and block damage from attacks, Shellder is much less effective than Lapras. It has only 30 HP, and its abilities can't protect it from effects like poison.

Krabby Lev. 20
Like Nidoran♀, Krabby has the ability to call other Krabby from your deck and place them on your Bench, one at a time. The Bench can be full of the little scuttlers in record time!

Club Master

12 Amy — Go-Go Rain Deck

Prize Cards: 6
Win: 2 Laboratory Boosters
Water Medal

(For Water Medal Autodeck Machine)

Once again, the Water Club champ seems to be much easier to defeat than the supposed lesser club members. You'll probably need to use a few delaying tactics of your own while you evolve benched Pikachu into Raichu, but if you can build up enough energy early in this duel, one or two Raichu will have no trouble flushing the competition down the proverbial drain.

Wartortle Lev. 22
Wartortle is one of the better fighters in Amy's arsenal. It can hit for 40 points of damage, but Amy often ends up using its damage-blocking Withdraw ability instead.

Lapras Lev. 31
If you think you can make room for another Full Heal card or two in your deck, do it. Lapras's Confuse Ray will be just as frustrating in this duel as it was in past competitions.

Seaking Lev. 28
This fishlike Pokémon doesn't seem to have much going for it, other than moderate energy costs. However, its attacks are pitifully weak for a Evolution 1 Pokémon.

Seadra Lev. 23
Seadra fares a little better than its waterborne cousin, Seaking. It can strike for 20 points of damage and, with a lucky coin toss, prevent any damage to itself next turn.

LIGHTNING CLUB

The sublime surroundings of the Water Club now give way to the bright lights and blaring sounds of the Lightning Club. Here you'll meet the many incarnations of Pikachu—but after a few rounds of card combat with it, it may not seem quite so cute and cuddly anymore!

Library

The texts in the Lightning Club collection explain some of the mysteries surrounding Lightning Pokémon, Energy Cards and playing Card Pop! via the infared ports. It's amazing what they're putting in books these days, isn't it?

Battle Center

PC   **Gift Center**

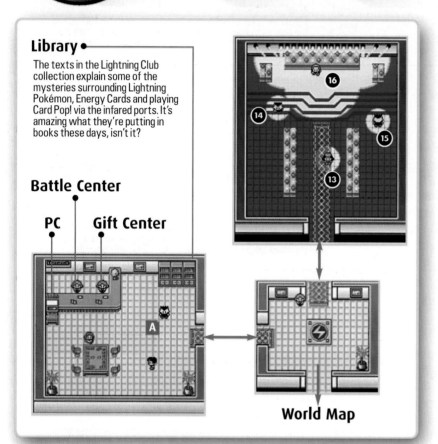

World Map

A Electrifying Trade

Are you more interested in trading or dueling wi[th] your cards? If you give a level-35 Electabuzz to th[e] collector, he'll give you a level-20 version of the cre[a]ture in return. The level-20 Electabuzz isn't as po[w]erful as its sibling, but it is much rarer.

Trade	Receive
Electabuzz Lev. 35	Electabuzz Lev. 20

Fight to the Finish

If you like to keep things simple, then you'll love this straightforward Fighting-type deck. The only really fancy maneuver in it is Rhydon's Ram attack, which hits for 50 points and switches the active Pokémon with one the defender chooses from the Bench. Beyond that, this deck is just about big hits and, at times, big energy costs. If you distribute your energy wisely, though, you'll be wearing the Lightning Medal in no time.

POKÉMON CARDS	LEVEL	
Sandshrew	12	3
➤ Sandslash	33	2
Diglet	8	3
➤ Dugtrio	36	2
Hitmonlee	30	3
Hitmonchan	33	3
Rhyhorn	18	3
➤ Rhydon	48	2

TRAINER CARDS	# OF CARDS
Bill	2
Energy Retrieval	2
Energy Search	2
Switch	2
Potion	2
Full Heal	2

Energy Cards	# OF CARDS
Fighting Energy	27

⓭ Jennifer — Pikachu Deck

Prize Cards: 4
Win: 2 Mystery Packs

Jennifer's deck is notable mostly as a novelty—as a dueling deck, it leaves a lot to be desired. Using various Pikachu is cute, but their abilities aren't varied or powerful enough to take you on by themselves. The only great worry here is Flyin' Pikachu, which is resistant to Fighting-types. There are ways around this obstacle, so it's not really necessary to include other Pokémon types in your deck.

Flying Pikachu Lev. 12
If Flying Pikachu or any other Fighting-resistant creature shows up in the arena, switch your active Pokémon with a Hitmonlee from your Bench. If you can't hit Pikachu, fight around it.

Surfing Pikachu Lev. 13
This fun-loving Pikachu would rather be breaking surfing records in Hawaii than breaking heads in the arena, but it can dish out 30 points of damage for just two Lightning Energy Cards.

Pikachu Lev. 16
You may never have another chance to see this rare version of Pikachu in action, so pay attention when it appears. It can cancel out 10 points of damage on the next turn and paralyze opponents.

⓮ Nicholas — Self Destruct Deck

Prize Cards: 4
Win: 2 Colosseum Boosters

As you might have guessed, one of Nicholas's favorite tactics is to blow up his Pokémon, taking yours along with them. There's little you can do to counteract this strategy, except to try to keep Nicholas from building up the energy he needs to trigger his creatures' explosive abilities. Having a couple of extra Energy Removal cards in your deck may help you deal with your incendiary opponent.

Koffing Lev. 13
Koffing's Foul Gas is one of the best basic attacks in the game. It does only 10 damage, but it will always poison or confuse the defending Pokémon unless it has some sort of special protection.

Magneton Lev. 35
If Magneton appears in the arena, just hope that you have a couple of Energy Removal Cards handy. Its Self Destruct will hit your active Pokémon for 100 damage and all Benched Pokémon for 20.

Geodude Lev. 16
Stone Barrage isn't the most reliable attack, but it can be devastating. The attacking player flips coins until tails appears. The attack does damage equal to the number of heads times 10.

⓯ Brandon — Power Generator Deck

Prize Cards: 4
Win: 2 Colosseum Boosters

Brandon's deck is stacked with heavy hitters, and Zapdos is his top contender. Zapdos is resistant to Fighting-types and has a whopping 90 HP, so unless you modify your deck with a few non-Fighting specimens, you may be in this bout for the long haul. We'd suggest using Pokémon that can use any type of energy, just so you won't have to worry about shortages at crucial times.

Pikachu Lev. 12
This version of Pikachu is nothing to be too excited about. It has moderate attack power, but if it's not careful, it can damage itself as well. Unless Brandon evolves it, don't worry.

Electabuzz Lev. 20
A sparkling personality is about all Electabuzz has going for it, at least when facing Fighting-types. Its attacks aren't powerful enough to overcome your creatures' resistance to electricity.

Zapdos Lev. 64
If all else fails, use Rhydon's Ram attack to hit Zapdos for 20 damage and send it to the Bench. Brandon will have to choose between paying retreat costs and allowing his new defender to be hammered.

Club Master — Zapping Deck

⓰ Isaac

Prize Cards: 6
Win: 2 Mystery Boosters
Lightning Medal

(For Lightning Medal Autodeck Machine)

Isaac has several strategies up his sleeve, and the one he uses depends on which cards he draws. If he's energy poor, he'll use Electabuzz or Magnemite to paralyze your active Pokémon as long as possible. If he's low on Pokémon, he'll use Kangaskhan to draw more cards. If he has electricity to spare, you can bet he'll use Self Destruct at least once during the bout.

Magnemite Lev. 13
Thunder Wave is an inexpensive attack that hits for 10 damage and can paralyze its target. If the paralyze effect fails, though, Magnemite won't survive long with just 40 HP.

Electabuzz Lev. 35
This Electabuzz is more powerful than its level-20 counterpart, but it does have its drawbacks. There's a chance that its Thunderpunch may backfire and damage Electabuzz itself.

Kangaskhan Lev. 40
Kangaskhan has 90 HP, and while its Comet Punch is expensive at four Energy Cards, it can hit for up to 80 points of damage. Try to wear it down while it's still on the Bench.

Magneton Lev. 28
In this deck, this is the Pokémon you'll fear. It's only slightly less powerful than the level-35 creature, still doing 80 damage to the active Pokémon and 20 damage to all others.

SCIENCE CLUB

The Science Club members are dedicated to different areas of Poké-mon research, and each is an expert in his or her field. If there's one thing you should learn from them, it's that experimentation and flexibility are very important when building your decks.

Library

Here you'll find shortcuts through the battle subscreens, the rules behind the confusion effect and inside info on Science-type Pokémon, which aren't a separate group but a subset of creatures from several different groups.

Battle Center

PC   **Gift Center**

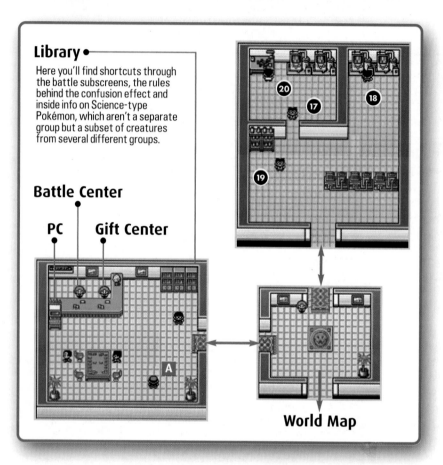

A

World Map

A Another Invitation

Once again, a club member will pass along a hint that Ishihara is looking to trade Pokémon with you. His reputation as a collector is impeccable—he probably has cards that no one else in the world has. Perhaps you should take time out from your busy schedule to visit his house.

Blinded with Science

As we mentioned, Science-type Pokémon come from different groups with different strengths and weaknesses. Few Pokémon, however, have a natural defense against Psychic-types, which form the backbone of the deck you see at the right. This deck is about keeping your foe off balance with paralyzing and confusing attacks, while also using special psychic powers to move damage counters (yours and your opponent's) from one Poké-mon to another. It's not a hard-hitting deck, but it is effective.

POKÉMON CARDS	LEVEL	# OF CARDS
Abra	10	4
➤ Kadabra	38	3
➤ Alakazam	42	2
Gastly	17	4
➤ Haunter	17	3
➤ Gengar	38	2
Drowzee	12	3
➤ Hypno	36	2

TRAINER CARDS	# OF CARDS
Bill	2
Mr. Fuji	2
Poké Ball	2
Potion	2
Full Heal	4

ENERGY CARDS	# OF CARDS
Psychic Energy	25

⑰ Joseph — Flyin' Pokémon Deck
Prize Cards: 4
Win: 2 Laboratory Boosters

In this game, flying ability really doesn't have any practical effect on combat, but Joseph's Pokémon have other formidable powers. The foremost of these is Pidgeotto's ability to force you to switch your active Pokémon with one from your Bench, one which he uses often. Be ready with lots of energy, Switch Cards and Pokémon with low retreat costs, or you may find yourself at your foe's mercy.

Pidgeot Lev. 40
For only three Energy Cards, Pidgeot can force your active Pokémon and all its attached cards back into your hand. You don't lose cards, but you lose precious time and defensive strength.

Golbat Lev. 29
Golbat is perfect as the first line of Joseph's defense. With the ability to heal its own wounds by using the life force of its target, it can survive almost indefinitely against low-level attacks.

Pidgeotto Lev. 36
Switching your active and Benched Pokémon is Pidgeotto's stock in trade. If Joseph brings Abra, Gastly or Haunter into the arena, however, it can retreat at no energy cost.

---

⑱ David — Lovely Nidoran Deck
Prize Cards: 4
Win: 2 Mystery Boosters

David's scheme is to overwhelm you with a flood of Nidoran ♀, Nidoran ♂ and their myriad descendants. If he's lucky enough to draw his Pokémon Breeder Cards early in the duel, he'll have his creatures evolved to Evolution 2 before you can say, "Pika!" This might be a good opportunity to try out a few Devolution Sprays or level-23 Mew cards. It will be an epic battle of science versus science!

Nidoqueen Lev. 43
Most versions of the Nidoran support each other one way or another, including Nidoqueen and Nidoking. For example, Nidoqueen's Boyfriends attack gains 20 damage for every Nidoking in play.

Nidoran ♂ Lev. 20
You can't have Nidoking without Nidoran ♂ first, and David has plenty of both. Nidoran ♂ doesn't have the Call for Family ability or a great attack, but David will evolve it quickly.

Meowth Lev. 15
If David can't field a Nidoran ♀, he'll place a Meowth in play if he can. It's not as good as Call for Family, but Meowth's Payday allows it to draw an extra card from the deck.

---

⑲ Erik — Poison Deck
Prize Cards: 4
Win: 2 Evolution Boosters

So far we've seen such wonders as flight and the process of accelerated evolution. Now comes a more sinister ability: the power to poison. This is a battle between Erik's poison powers and your paralyzing/sleep-inducing attacks. Besides Full Heal Cards, you should also carry Mr. Fuji Cards. If you can't heal a Pokémon, retreat it and then send it back to the deck, rather than let it be defeated.

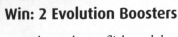

Koffing Lev. 13
You've encountered Koffing before, and you know what it can do. The only question is whether you'll be able to knock it out before it can unleash its powers of confusion and paralysis.

Kakuna Lev. 23
Kakuna can cancel out all damage against it, but it can't protect itself from other battle effects. Perhaps you should think about launching a poisonous assault of your own...

Ekans Lev. 10
Ekans's Spit Poison attack does no base damage at all, but its Wrap attack hits for 20 points and has the potential to paralyze its target. Not great, but not bad for a basic Pokémon.

Club Master
⑳ Rick — Wonders of Science Deck
Prize Cards: 4
Win: 2 Mystery Boosters
Science Medal
(For Science Medal Autodeck Machine)

Here's your chance to earn a PhD in puttin' the smack down on your opponent. Rick's deck is based less on the "wonders" of science than the havoc that it can cause. For all his Pokémon's powers, though, he doesn't seem to have a particularly organized strategy. As for you, you can return to the original strategy of keeping your foes off balance and manipulating damage.

Grimer Lev. 17
Rick likes to open bouts with Grimer, because it can block up to 20 damage points per turn. It can hold up against basic Pokémon for an annoyingly long while.

Koffing Lev. 13
The fact that you're seeing Koffing so often in duels is a testament to how effective it is in combat. Once again, just try to take it out before it can evolve into Weezing.

Mewtwo Lev. 60
Mewtwo can hold off even the most powerful Pokémon, but for a price. By discarding one Energy Card, Mewtwo can block all damage and combat effects against itself on the next turn.

Weezing Lev. 27
If you think Rick is about to use Self Destruct, use Gengar's Curse power to move your opponent's damage counters around so that at least one other enemy Pokémon is defeated.

PSYCHIC CLUB

Psychic Club members believe that the powers of the mind far surpass those of the body, and they're prepared to test that theory in combat. In truth, Psychic-type Pokémon are among the most powerful, so don't write your victory speech until you have the Psychic Medal in hand.

Library

Forewarned is forearmed, as the saying goes, so learn as much as you can about your opponents before going into battle. Here you can learn about Psychic-types, attacks that send Pokémon to sleep and other special Pokémon Powers.

Battle Center

PC   ### Gift Center

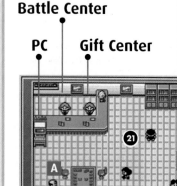

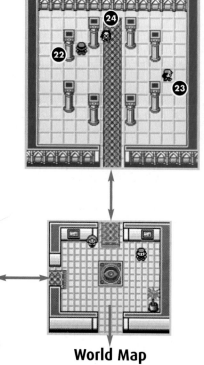

World Map

A Grudge Match?

This spry senior citizen will give you a rare Mewtw card if you defeat the Psychic Club champ in a due We don't know if he has some sort of grudge again: Murray or if he's just trying to encourage you, but ou advice is not to look a gift Pokémon in the mouth...

Receive
Mewtwo Lev. 60

Psychic Hotline

This deck takes advantage of the few Psychic-type and Colorless-type Pokémon that can resist Psychic-type powers. Jigglypuff and Kangaskhan are best for delaying your opponent during the opening rounds, while most of your offensive power will come from Wigglytuff and Kangaskhan. We also like Dragonair for its ability to remove Energy Cards from enemy Pokémon. If you wish, you can even try an all-Colorless deck, substituting the Psychic-types for Meowth (level 15), Persian (level 25) and Tauros (level 32).

POKéMON CARDS	LEVEL	# OF CARDS
Gastly	17	3
➤Haunter	22	2
➤Gengar	38	1
Jigglypuff	14	4
➤Wigglytuff	36	3
Kangaskhan	40	3
Dratini	10	3
➤Dragonair	33	2

TRAINER CARDS	# OF CARDS
Bill	2
Energy Removal	2
Switch	2
Gust of Wind	2
Potion	2
Full Heal	4

ENERGY CARDS	# OF CARDS
Psychic Energy	21
Double Colorless Energy	4

㉑ Robert — Ghost Deck

Prize Cards: 4
Win: 2 Evolution Boosters

Robert has several Psychic-resistant Pokémon as well, so you'll have to field more of your Colorless-types in this duel. He'll try to rush a lot of Pokémon onto his bench, sometimes even before he has the energy to power them up. A Gust of Wind would come in handy, possibly stranding an energy-less Pokémon in the arena. Gengar's Bench-hitting Dark Mind would also help in this situation.

Meowth Lev. 15
You've seen this sneaky specimen before, and you know that Robert will be using its Payday ability to pull Pokémon out of his deck. Luckily for you, Meowth doesn't have nine lives.

Zubat Lev. 10
Zubat isn't resistant to Psychic powers, and it has only 40 HP. Despite the fact that it can remove damage counters from itself, it shouldn't be able to last long.

Gengar Lev. 38
It will be a race to see who can field Gengar first. If your opponent uses Gengar's Curse to shift damage to a Benched Pokémon, you can use Gengar's Dark Mind or a Gust of Wind Card in response.

㉒ Daniel — Nap Time Deck

Prize Cards: 4
Win: 2 Evolution Boosters

As you might guess, Daniel is hoping he'll be able to send your Pokémon to the Land of Nod for the duration of this battle. If you add a couple more Full Heal cards to your deck, you should be able to muddle through just fine. Daniel has many of the same Pokémon you have in your deck, including Haunter and Wigglytuff, so we'll see if you can take it as well as you dish it out.

Exeggcute Lev. 14
Daniel will use Exeggcute's Hypnosis to stall the match and build up his Pokémon. Hypnosis can't damage your Pokémon, though, so you can take advantage of the pause in the action, too.

Haunter Lev. 17
This Haunter is different from the one we've recommended for you. Its Nightmare attack does only 10 damage, but unlike your Haunter's Dream Eater attack, the target doesn't have to be asleep.

Wigglytuff Lev. 36
This Wigglytuff, on the other hand, is the same as yours. Once again, you'll probably need a bit of pluck and a bit of luck to win the Pokémon arms race.

㉓ Stephanie — Strange Power Deck

Prize Cards: 4
Win: 2 Laboratory Boosters

One of Stephanie's favorite strategies may seem familiar to you: using Hypno to reach around your active Pokémon and strike at your Benched defenders. Wait as long as possible, then use a Mr. Fuji Card to return the wounded Pokémon (and all the cards attached to it) to your deck. Don't do this too quickly, or you'll just give Stephanie a chance to attack another defender sooner.

Mr. Mime Lev. 28
You may be wondering how to counteract Mr. Mime's ability to cancel out all attacks over 30 points of damage. Simply hit him for 10 or 20 damage at a time, or put him to sleep first.

Hypno Lev. 36
Hypno has the same Dark Mind attack as Gengar has, as well as the gift of Prophecy. This ability allows the player to look at either deck and arrange the top three cards in any order.

Slowpoke Lev. 9
In Slowpoke's case, the best offense is a good defense. Its Amnesia power causes no damage, but it will make your active Pokémon forget how to use one attack on the next turn.

Club Master

Strange Psychic Deck

㉔ Murray

Prize Cards: 6
Win: 2 Laboratory Boosters
Psychic Medal

(For Psychic Medal Autodeck Machine)

The battle with Murray may be less about overpowering him and more about outlasting him. He sometimes retreats or uses Pokémon Center (discard all damage counters from all of your Pokémon with damage counters, then discard all Energy Cards attached to those Pokémon) when he doesn't need to, wasting energy in the process. You may just wear him down until he has no power left.

Alakazam Lev. 42
Murray also likes to use Alakazam's Damage Swap power to move damage counters among his creatures. He won't think he's so clever if you respond with Dark Mind.

Mr. Mime Lev. 28
Mr. Mime has a resistance to Colorless-type Pokémon, so you may need to include a few more Psychic-types in your deck for this duel. This mute mutant can be a very effective defense.

Chansey Lev. 55
If Murray becomes desperate, he won't hesitate to use Chansey's Double Edge attack. This works the same as the Self Destruct attacks you've seen in past battles.

Energy Removal
This battle will see the both of you trying to throw away the other's Energy Cards. You can use a couple Energy Removal Cards of your own or use Dragonair's Hyper Beam.

FIGHTING CLUB

If you wish to challenge the members of the Fighting Club, you'll have to find them first. Mitch's lieutenants are training at the Rock, Grass and Fire Clubs. Once you beat them, they'll return to their home club, where you'll be able to meet Mitch in honorable combat.

Library

Fighting Club members believe that gaining wisdom is the true path of a warrior. You can start that journey right here, learning more about Fighting-type Pokémon and special Pokémon Powers.

Battle Center

PC   **Gift Center**

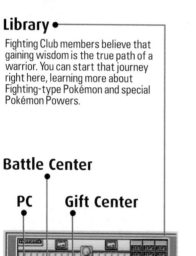

World Map

A Pick a Pikachu

Here's an anxious collector who will gladly take Graveler in exchange for one of the more unusual versions of Pikachu around. After you seal that deal, he'll also put other cards into safekeeping for you, if you wish. Will he keep them permanently, though?

Trade	Receive
Graveler Lev. 26 	Pikachu Lev. 16 
Omastar Lev. 32	
Parasect Lev. 28 x2	
Weezing Lev. 27	

Psychic Solution

Once again, the Psychic-types and Colorless-types will come to your rescue, with several flying creatures taking the lead. For more Psychic power, swap Abra, Kadabra and Alakazam for some of your Colorless-types. If you'd like to be really daring, add a third type of Pokémon to your deck. In our section on deck building, we recommended against using three-type decks until you had more experience. Considering what you're up against here, now may be the time to try it. Try substituting two Hitmonchan and two Hitmonlee for one set of your Colorless-type creatures. If you do this, use 11 Psychic Energy, 11 Fighting Energy, 4 Double Colorless Energy and 2 Energy Search Cards.

POKéMON CARDS	LEVEL	# OF CARDS
Gastly	17	4
► Haunter	17	3
► Gengar	38	2
Pidgey	8	4
► Pidgeotto	36	3
Spearow	13	4
► Fearow	27	3

TRAINER CARDS	# OF CARDS
Bill	2
Poké Ball	2
Energy Removal	3
Switch	2
Potion	3

ENERGY CARDS	# OF CARDS
Psychic Energy	21
Double Colorless Energy	4

25 Chris — Muscle for Brains Deck

Prize Cards: 4
Win: 2 Evolution Boosters

You'll find Chris in the lounge of the Rock Club. If you're wondering what kind of opponent he is, the name of his deck says it all. There's not much to deal with here, except for a lot of punching and kicking. If your deck is heavy with Psychic-types, however, beware of Tauros. As you know by now, this creature is Psychic-resistant and can hold its own in the arena without a problem.

Tauros Lev. 32
If you are unlucky enough to encounter Tauros, use Gastly or Abra to hold it at bay while you prepare a Colorless-type for battle. Spearow or Fearow would probably give Tauros a run for its money.

Hitmonlee Lev. 30
If you're using Hitmonlee's Stretch Kick attack, resistance and weakness are not taken into account when tallying the damage. That could work for or against you, depending on the situation.

Hitmonchan Lev. 33
This pugilistic Pokémon is one of the more economical Fighting-types, delivering 20 points of damage with just one Energy Card and 40 points of damage for three cards.

26 Michael — Heated Battle Deck

Prize Cards: 4
Win: 2 Colosseum Boosters

If you want to see what it's like to use three different types of Pokémon in one deck, here's your chance. Michael uses a combination of Fighting-type, Fire-type and Electric-type Pokémon in his Heated Battle deck. We didn't include any Full Heal Cards in the deck shown on the previous page, but you may encounter a paralyzing attack in this duel, so add a couple of them now.

Magmar Lev. 24
On the one hand, this version of Magmar doesn't have a poisonous attack. On the other, this is the version that can strike for up to 50 points of damage. We're not sure which one is worse!

Electabuzz Lev. 35
This is the Pokémon that prompted us to add a couple of Full Heal Cards to the current deck. If it shows up in the arena, you can bet that Michael will use its paralyzing Thundershock attack.

Magmar Lev. 24
Both Flareon and Magmar have devastating Flamethrower attacks, but Magmar's is cheaper and nearly as powerful. At 50 points of damage, this attack is worth the one Energy Card you must discard.

27 Jessica — Love to Battle Deck

Prize Cards: 4
Win: 2 Colosseum Boosters

Jessica has a passion for battle, but if she wants to play in the big leagues, she'll have to come up with a better deck than this. She's built her strategy around a mix of Fighting-types and Colorless-types, but none of them are particularly heavy hitters. Perhaps after you've defeated her once, she'll learn from her experience—or perhaps you can defeat her again easily and earn even more booster packs!

Raticate Lev. 41
The only big roadblocks you'll encounter here are Rattata and Raticate, which have a resistance to Psychic-types. Use any Fighting-types or Colorless-types in your deck to plow through them.

Dodrio Lev. 28
As long as Dodrio is on his Bench, Jessica will pay lower retreat costs. She'll need this special power, once you start whaling big time on her active Pokémon.

Defender
Jessica also packs a few Defender Cards in her deck. While they can be useful, they can't make up for weak or non-evolved Pokémon. As the saying goes, the best defense, is a good—well, you know.

Club Master
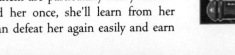

28 Mitch — First Strike Deck

Prize Cards: 6
Win: 2 Laboratory Boosters
Fighting Medal
(For Fighting Medal Autodeck Machine)

Now here's an opponent worthy of your fighting mettle! As the name of his deck implies, Mitch will strike quickly, usually leading off with a Machop. Field a Gastly first if you can, to give yourself some time to prepare other defenders. Focus on using any paralyzing, poisonous or sleep-inducing attacks to help chip away at your opponents' high HP ratings.

Machop Lev. 20
Machop is perfect as a first-strike weapon, using only one Fighting Energy Card for its Low Kick attack, allowing it to go on the offensive immediately.

Hitmonchan Lev. 33
As much as you liked using this Pokémon in your deck, you'll hate it when its powers are turned against you. It, too, has lots of power for its energy costs.

Hitmonlee Lev. 30
The only thing about Hitmonlee that will work in your favor is that its most powerful attack requires three Energy Cards. Can you say, "Energy Removal?"

PlusPower
The difference between surviving an attack and going down in defeat is often just one damage counter, and the PlusPower Card can mean all the difference in the world.

ROCK CLUB

If you know the old saying about being caught between a rock and a hard place, we think you'll agree that this final club is the proverbial hard place. Who would have thought, though, that the "rock" would turn out to be a type of Pokémon!

Library

Essays on Rock-type Pokémon and Pokémon evolution are just two of the interesting volumes found on these shelves. In the Pokémon Trading Card Game, the Rock-type is actually a subset of the Fighting-type and not a separate grouping.

Battle Center

PC   Gift Center

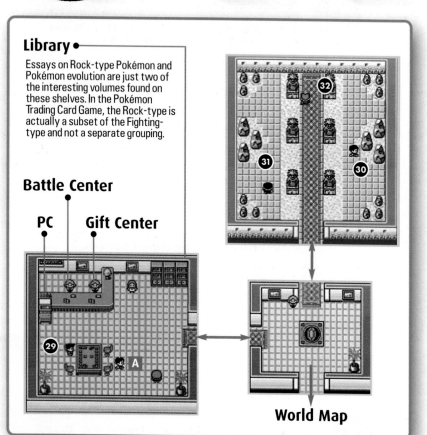

World Map

A Seal the Deal

It seems that you're not the only one interested i trading with Ishihara. In fact, this collector is thin ing of making an offer for one of his rarest cards. you haven't visited Mr. Ishihara yet, you'd better dro by his house before you miss your opportunity.

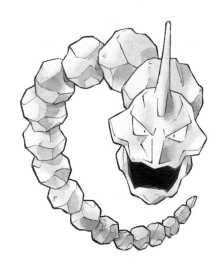

Greener Pastures

Rock-types are tough, but rest assured that rocks can be broken, and Grass-types are the right tools for the job. A few Caterpie, Metapod and Koffing can provide early defense, while you use your Poké Ball and Pokémon Breeder Cards to evolve your Benched creatures quickly. Later in a duel, Venusaur's Energy Transform and Butterfree's Whirlwind will keep your opponent off balance. For variety, you could substitute the Nidoran♂ line or the Bellsprout line for one of the groups in the deck, or maybe even throw in two or three Scyther.

POKéMON CARDS	LEVEL	# OF CARDS
Bulbasaur	13	4
➤ Ivysaur	20	3
➤ Venusaur	67	2
Caterpie	13	4
➤ Metapod	21	3
➤ Butterfree	28	3
Koffing	13	2

TRAINER CARDS	# OF CARDS
Bill	2
Pokémon Breeder	3
Energy Removal	2
Poké Ball	3
Potion	2
Full Heal	2

ENERGY CARDS	# OF CARDS
Psychic Energy	21
Double Colorless Energy	4

㉙ Matthew ⟨Hard Pokémon Deck⟩
Prize Cards: 4
Win: 2 Mystery Boosters

Matthew sometimes seems to have difficulty drawing anything but basic Pokémon from his deck early in a duel. With the Grass-types' natural advantage over Rock-types, it's not unusual to claim all four prizes before he even knocks out one of your defenders. In fact, we've won several duels with just a single Bulbasaur or a lone Koffing! Of course, luck can run the other way, too...

Cubone Lev. 13
Cubone's Snivel can block up to 20 points of damage on the next turn. This will block all attack damage from Caterpie and Koffing, but not the paralysis, confusion or poison they deliver.

Onix Lev. 12
Matthew often uses Onix as a glorified wall. With its damage-blocking abilities and 90 HP, you may have to remove its Energy Cards before you can even think about making a dent in it.

Geodude Lev. 16
Geodude's Stone Barrage attack isn't very consistent, but it is cheap, and it has the potential to knock out even the toughest opponent in one turn. Energy Removal to the rescue!

 ㉚ Ryan ⟨Excavation Deck⟩
Prize Cards: 3
Win: 2 Evolution Boosters

The most significant thing about Ryan's deck is that it includes the Mysterious Fossil card. Though it is considered a Trainer Card, it is played as if it were a Pokémon card. This item can actually be evolved into one of several true Pokémon, including Aerodactyl, Kabuto and, Ryan's favorite, Omanyte. If he must, Ryan will neglect his active Pokémon to ensure that Omanyte is fully powered.

Hitmonchan Lev. 33
By now, Hitmonchan is a familiar face to you. Though its flashing fists may give you pause, you shouldn't have trouble delivering a knockout blow within two or three rounds.

Cubone Lev. 13
Cubone is also a common fixture in Ryan's deck. While Cubone is hardly ever a cause for great concern, you'll have more of a fight on your hands if Ryan manages to evolve it into Marowak.

Mysterious Fossil
Omanyte is Ryan's favorite Evolution 1 for the Mysterious Fossil. Its Pokémon Power forces you to reveal your hand to Ryan, making it easy for him to anticipate your moves.

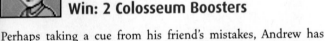

 ㉛ Andrew ⟨Blistering Pokémon Deck⟩
Prize Cards: 4
Win: 2 Colosseum Boosters

Perhaps taking a cue from his friend's mistakes, Andrew has included several Fire-type Pokémon in his deck, including Jynx and Ponyta. Your Grass-types are vulnerable to fire-based attacks, so you may want to swap out a few of them for some Water-type creatures. You can still win with the deck we suggested, but you'll need a few lucky coin tosses to help you along.

Rhyhorn Lev. 18
Rhyhorn's Leer ability, which can stop opponents from even launching an attack, makes it a popular choice among many players. At 70 HP, it's unusually tough for a basic Pokémon.

Jynx Lev. 23
With your weakness adding extra damage to its attacks, the so-so Jynx will suddenly gain a new measure of respect when facing your Grass-type Pokémon. Have fun trying to put out its fire!

Ponyta Lev. 10
If you have only basic Grass-types on your bench and in the arena, the arrival of Ponyta may signal the beginning of the end for you. Potions and Energy Removals can only help in this situation!

 **Club Master** ⟨Rock Crusher Deck⟩
㉜ Gene
Prize Cards: 6
Win: 2 Mystery Boosters
Rock Medal
(For Rock Medal Autodeck Machine)

Gene is your final opponent before facing the Pokémon card game masters, and he's determined to make you earn your place in the championship bouts. Onix or Rhyhorn often leads the charge for him, followed by Geodude, Dugtrio and more. Despite their weakness to Grass-types, the evolved forms of Gene's Rock-types can withstand a lot of punishment, thanks to their high HP.

Diglett Lev. 8
In a duel between one of your basic Grass-types and Diglett, Diglett stands little chance. If Gene can evolve it into Dugtrio, however, the tables will turn very quickly.

Graveler Lev. 29
Another mainstay of Gene's deck, Graveler can hold its own against most of your basic Pokémon and even some of your Evolution 1 creatures, especially if it has the first strike.

Rhyhorn Lev. 18
At one Energy Card, Rhyhorn's Leer ability is a terrific bargain. But Gene rarely uses its less economical Horn Attack.

Onix Lev. 12
Onix is another one-trick Pokémon for Gene, used mostly for its Rock Throw attack. Onix has so much HP, Gene rarely feels compelled to use its Harden defensive ability.

FURTHER ADVENTURES

There's more to your quest than dueling the members of the card Clubs. While you train for your showdown with the card masters, you'll participate in two local competitions and meet several interesting characters, including a strange music man named Imakuni? and your rival for the Legendary Pokémon Cards, the ever-persistent Ronald.

Library

Besides serving as the arena for local card tournaments, the Challenge Hall also houses a public library. Interested patrons can read up on Colorless-type Pokémon, including those that have birdlike and dragonlike characteristics.

Battle Center

PC   Gift Center

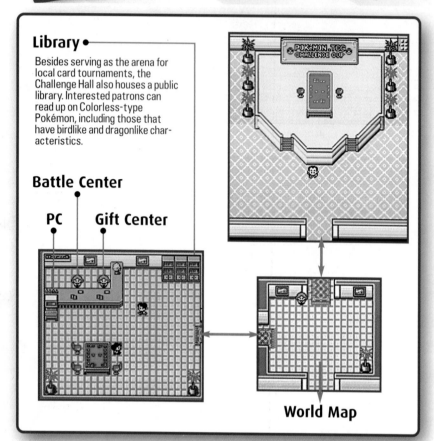

World Map

Challenge Cup

If you'd like to sharpen your card-playing skills even further, visit the Challenge Hall arena between bouts at the various clubs. Once or twice during your adventure, the Challenge Cup tournament will be held, pitting local experts against one another. If you arrive at the right time, you'll be invited to participate. If you win the first tournament, you'll earn a rare Mewtwo card. If you come out on top at the second competition, you'll walk away with bragging rights and a special Mew card. The competitions are held at random times, so there's no guarantee you'll be able to participate. If you do, it will be a good chance to examine other players' decks and strategies.

Mewtwo Lev. 60   Mew Lev. 8

Imakuni?

Prize Cards: 6
Win: one of every booster

No one will be able to tell you much about Imakuni?, the strange but talented card player you'll meet in different Club lounges from time to time. He says he's a musician by trade, but that doesn't explain his mouse-eared costume or his wild playing style. In any case, his deck (shown at the right) is challenging if a bit scatter-brained, with a mix of Water-type, Psychic-type and Colorless-type creatures. If you play against him often enough, he may eventually give you a promotion card featuring...him!

POKÉMON CARDS	LEVEL	# OF CARDS
Psyduck	15	4
➤ Golduck	27	3
Slowpoke	9	2
Slowpoke	18	2
➤ Slowbro	26	3
Drowzee	12	4
➤ Hypno	36	3
Farfetch'd	20	4
Imakuni?		4
Maintenance		2
Pokémon Flute		2
Gambler		1
Water Energy		10
Psychic Energy		16

Farfetch'd Lev. 20
Farfetch'd is one of the more unusual Pokémon you'll eve encounter. Its Leek Slap attack is relatively powerful at damage points, but once it's used, it can't be used again.

Psyduck Lev. 15
Looking like it has a lot on its mind, Psyduck can give you a Headache that prevents you from using any Trainer Cards the next turn. Oooo, that's gotta hurt!

Slowbro Lev. 26
Slowbro's Pokémon Power is called Strange Behavior, which fits in perfectly with this crowd. Using Strange Behavior, this dull-witted Pokémon can absorb damage from its fellows.

Imakuni? Card

The Imakuni? card is an interesting collectible, to be sur If you play it, though, you'll succeed only in confusing yo active Pokémon. Imakuni? himself seems to like it—but that's not saying very much!

Ronald

The lure of the Legendary Cards is strong, and many players would do anything, even give up their entire collections, to own those most precious and powerful cards. Indeed, many players hope to win those cards from the Pokémon card masters, but only one will succeed. While you're certainly in the running, there is one other who could prove worthy: your rival, Ronald. Your first encounter with him will be after you win your second medal, the second will be after you win your fifth medal, and the third will be at the second Challenge Cup.

First Encounter Deck

Prize Cards: 6
Win: Jigglypuff Lev. 12

After you win your second medal, Ronald will appear in the Club lobby and your duel will begin automatically. Be sure to modify your deck and save your game, if necessary, before you go out to meet him. In this first battle Ronald will use mostly basic Pokémon.

 Charmander Lev. 10
By now, you're more than familiar with this fiery little fiend. It won't take much to put a damper on its enthusiasm, but just be on the lookout for its Evolution 1 and Evolution 2 counterparts.

Cubone Lev. 13
Cubone can boost its Rage attack by adding 10 points for every damage counter it has on itself. With just 40 HP, though, it won't be around to use that trick more than once or twice.

Squirtle Lev. 8
With a face like that, Squirtle seems more friend than foe, no matter which side it's on. Ronald is more likely to use its damage-blocking Withdraw than its Bubble attack.

Second Encounter Deck

Prize Cards: 6
Win: Super Energy Retrieval

Ronald will challenge you again after you've won your fifth medal. His training will show in his improved deck and more sophisticated strategies. Once again, it would be wise to modify your deck before you talk to him. Your best bets will be Psychic-type and/or Fighting-type Pokémon.

Electabuzz Lev. 35
Electabuzz is more powerful than many other basic Pokémon, but its electrical abilities are unstable. A bad coin toss can result in Electabuzz giving itself a bad shock.

Hitmonchan Lev. 33
One of the most straightforward Pokémon, there's nothing particularly clever or sophisticated about Hitmonchan. Like Electabuzz, it has higher HP than the average basic Pokémon.

Tauros Lev. 32
By now, the strategy in this deck is obvious: Use basic Pokémon that are as powerful as more advanced creatures. It gives Ronald fast, powerful attacks with no evolution required!

Third Encounter Deck

Prize Cards: 6
Win: Jigglypuff Lev. 12

Ronald will really show his fighting mettle in your third meeting. With more powerful and varied cards at his command, he may prove strong enough to challenge even the card masters. The only thing that could use improvement is his bad attitude—he won't win friends here!

Geodude Lev. 16
This Pokémon has given you trouble before, and your reunion promises to be no happier than your first meeting. Hope that you'll have a Pokémon in the arena that can block all damage.

Magmar Lev. 31
If Magmar's damage-blocking Smokescreen is successful on one turn, it can use its poisoning Smog on the next without fear of retaliation—a deadly combination that you should fear!

Scyther Lev. 25
If Scyther uses its Swords Dance ability successfully on one turn, you know that a 60-point Slash attack will be coming the next. Again, a damage-blocking ability would be helpful.

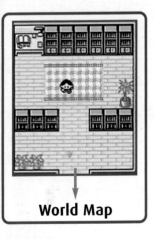

World Map

Ishihara

Though his dueling days are long past, Ishihara remains as enthusiastic as ever about Pokémon cards. He's happy to share his passion for his hobby with you, and he'll be very generous with you if you remember to visit from time to time. Over time, he'll ask you for a Clefable, a Ditto and a Chansey. In return, he'll give you three rare Pikachu cards (two Surfing and one Flying), which you might remember from your duels in the Lightning Club.

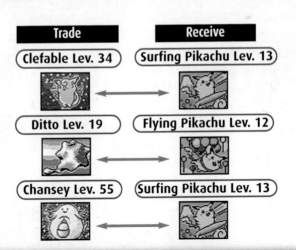

Trade	Receive
Clefable Lev. 34	Surfing Pikachu Lev. 13
Ditto Lev. 19	Flying Pikachu Lev. 12
Chansey Lev. 55	Surfing Pikachu Lev. 13

POKéMON DOME

You've paid your dues in the card clubs, and now it's time to reap the rewards of all your hard work. You've proven that you're worthy to challenge the greatest Poké- mon card game players in the world; now you must prove that you're worthy to inherit the four Pokémon cards of legend: Moltres, Articuno, Zapdos and Dragonite.

Legendary Autodeck Machine •

You won't be able to use this Autodeck Machine until your sec- ond visit to the Pokémon Dome. As soon as you take all the Legendary Cards, you'll be transported auto- matically to Mason Laboratory. To use the machine, you must defeat the masters a second time and then use the machine before you claim your tournament prize.

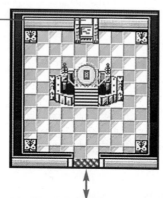

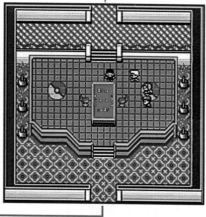

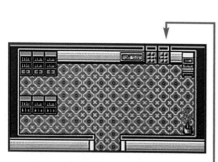

Eye on the Prize

This what you've been working toward since day one, and your chance to claim the rarest of cards is finally here. Once you enter the domed arena, there's no turning back. You'll meet the masters one at a time, and you'll have a chance between bouts to save your progress and modify your deck. If you lose just one duel, you'll be tossed out of the arena. You may challenge the masters again, but you'll have to start over from the first duel.

Dedicated Decks

Since you'll be able to modify your deck between duels, you won't have to worry about creating a single "super deck" to take on the masters. Like your past oppo- nents, the masters tend to specialize in just one or two Pokémon types in their decks. Using your previous decks as guides, you can tailor a deck specifically for each master. For example, Courtney uses mainly Fire-type cards, so enter the dome with a Water-type deck. Before you move on to the duel with Steve, create a Fighting-type deck to short-circuit his Lightning-type creatures, and so on. Be sure to include more powerful cards or cards you haven't had a chance to use before. You can save your progress, so don't be afraid to experiment.

Moltres Lev. 37

Articuno Lev. 37

Zapdos Lev. 68

Dragonite Lev. 41

Courtney
[Legendary Moltres Deck]
Mistress of Fire
Prize Cards: 6

One of Courtney's favorite tactics is to use Pokémon Trader to draw Moltres or another needed creature from her deck. She'll then use Moltres's Pokémon Power to draw a Fire Energy Card as well. With this combo move, she can keep her Bench well stocked, and no matter which Pokémon you place into the arena, she'll likely have a good response for you. This duel can drag on for quite some time, so be patient and cautious.

Moltres Lev. 37
This version of Moltres is easily more powerful than the level-35 version you've encountered before. Its Dive Bomb causes less damage, but its Pokémon Power makes it invaluable.

Ninetales Lev. 35
Besides hitting you for up to 80 damage points, your foe will use this Ninetales to force you to return any Pokémon in your hand to your deck and then draw new ones at random.

Arcanine Lev. 45
Arcanine's attacks are expensive, either in energy costs or in damage that Arcanine must take to use them. Courtney, however, won't hesitate to use them, if they result in knockout blows.

Steve
[Legendary Zapdos Deck]
Master of Lightning
Prize Cards: 6

Compared to Steve's Pokémon, your Fighting-type creatures may seem a little underpowered at first glance. If you select Pokémon like those in the Sandshrew line and the Diglett line, however, their natural resistance to Lighting-types will help increase your defensive capability. Hitmonchan and Hitmonlee don't have lightning-type resistance, but they'd be good additions to your arsenal, anyway.

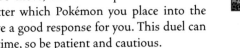

Zapdos Lev. 68
This Zapdos has one of the most economical attacks in the game (a hair-raising 70 points of damage for only three Lightning Energy Cards), but the damage can hit friend or foe at random.

Electabuzz Lev. 35
Despite the big differences in their attacks and HP, the seemingly lowly Sandshrew is more than a match for Electabuzz. Electabuzz's normal attacks can barely overcome Sandshrew's resistance.

Zapdos Lev. 64
You may see this version of Zapdos late in the duel. Its energy costs are high, but so too are its HP and attack damage. Even if he's energy poor, Steve may play this card as a last-ditch effort.

Jack
[Legendary Articuno Deck]
Master of Ice
Prize Cards: 6

A mix of mainly Lightning-type Pokémon with a few Fighting-types will serve you well in the battle with cool Jack. It would have to be a cold day in you-know-where for Jack just to hand the victory to you; and yet, he seems to be too reliant on Energy Retrieval Cards and is energy poor too much of the time. Perhaps some Energy Removal Cards would be in order for your deck...

Articuno Lev. 37
If Articuno is put into play during a regular turn (not during the initial setup), a coin is flipped. If it comes up heads, the opposing active Pokémon is paralyzed. What a chilling thought!

Dewgong Lev. 42
This happy-go-lucky Pokémon will prove to be a formidable foe. Its Aurora Beam costs just three Energy Cards for 50 points of damage. Add another energy to use the paralyzing Ice Beam.

Chansey Lev. 55
Chansey's Double Edge attack is similar to Self Destruct, but it doesn't knock out the opponent automatically. If Chansey is at full health when it uses Double Edge, it will be left with 40 HP.

Rod
[Legendary Dragon Deck]
Grandmaster
Prize Cards: 6

Rod is the grand master of this elite group of card players, and it shows in his diverse and devastating deck. Much of his early defense comes from very different creatures, like Magikarp, Lapras and Kangaskhan, while Gyarados and Dragonite form the backbone of his main Pokémon force. We suggest using Grass-types and lightning-types to wrap up this duel in a flash.

Dragonite Lev. 41
Dragonite's Healing Wind can remove up to two damage counters from each friendly Pokémon, but this power can be used only on the turn Dragonite is played. Think of it as emergency first aid!

Gyarados Lev. 41
Magikarp takes a huge leap in HP and attack power when it evolves into Gyarados. It's resistant to Fighting-types but weak against Grass-types.

Lapras Lev. 31
With 80 HP, it's no wonder that this basic Pokémon is one of Rod's favorite frontline defenders. Its attacks, however, are relatively weak, striking for up to only 20 damage.

Final Showdown
Ronald
Prize Cards: 6

Now that you've defeated Rod and the rest of the masters, you have one more contender to face before you can claim the Legendary Cards for yourself. That's right; it's none other than your rival, Ronald. The cocky kid has become a cunning card shark, and, worse yet, he'll be allowed to use the Legendary Cards against you in this duel. It's time to put your deck-building skills to the test, and see if your strategies can overcome Ronald's raw power!

Legendary Ronald

POKéMON CARDS	LEVEL	# OF CARDS
Kangaskhan	40	2
Eevee	12	4
Flareon	22	1
Vaporeon	29	1
Jolteon	24	1
Dratini	10	4
Dragonair	33	3
Dragonite	41	2
Moltres	37	2
Articuno	37	1
Zapdos	68	1
Professor Oak		1
Bill		3
Pokémon Trader		1
Pokémon Breeder		2
Energy Removal		3
Scoop Up		3
Gambler		1
Fire Energy		20
Double Colorless Energy		4

Double Danger

In most cases up until now, we've recommended using just one or two types of Pokémon in a deck. If there were a second type, it was often Colorless, so that energy wouldn't be a problem. For this bout, though, we recommend using Water-types, Fighting-types and Colorless-types. We chose Golduck and Dragonair specifically for their energy-stealing powers, and Hitmonlee for its ability to strike Benched Pokémon. The others are there for their raw hitting power and for balancing the energy needed in the deck.

POKéMON CARDS	LEVEL	# OF CARDS
Psyduck	15	3
➤ Golduck	27	2
Seel	12	3
➤ Dewgong	42	2
Dratini	10	3
➤ Dragonair	33	2
Hitmonlee	30	3
Hitmonchan	33	3

TRAINER CARDS	# OF CARDS
Bill	2
Energy Search	2
Energy Retrieval	2
Switch	2
Poké Ball	2
Potion	2
Full Heal	2

ENERGY CARDS	# OF CARDS
Water Energy	12
Fighting Energy	10
Double Colorless Energy	3

Postscript Challenge Cup Prizes

After you win the Legendary Cards and become one of the Pokémon Trading Card Game elite, there will still be other challenges to overcome. Dr. Mason will build a tournament computer for you to use, and the Challenge Cup competitions will go on. Some of the fun and rare cards that you can win at the Challenge Cup are listed below.

Arcanine Lev. 34

Mewtwo Lev. 60

Surfing Pikachu Lev. 13

Electabuzz Lev. 20

Pikachu Lev. 16

Mew Lev. 8

Mewtwo Lev. 60

Surfing Pikachu Lev. 13

Jigglypuff Lev. 12

Flying Pikachu Lev. 12

Slowpoke Lev. 9

Pikachu Lev. 16

Super Energy Retrieval

DECK DATA

There are over 200 cards to keep track of in the Pokémon Trading Card Game. Some are very common, while others are quite rare. We even have info on the special cards that exist only in the Game Boy Pak! For your reference, we also list the decks that the Autodeck Machines will build for you—if you have the right cards.

DATA CARD KEY

The following pages show all of the cards in this game, including the special promotional cards that are exclusive to the Game Boy. The cards are listed by type, beginning with Pokémon cards, followed by Trainer Cards, Energy Cards and the exclusive cards. These data will be your most valuable resources for building decks and creating strategies.

Pokémon ID Number and Rarity

This number is the Pokémon's identification number. The symbols indicate how many copies of this card are in the game. One black dot means it will be easy to find and win this card, while a star means it is a rare card and will be difficult to find.

● MANY   ◆ FEW   ★ RARE

Card ID Number

These are the ID numbers used in the real-world card game. For example, this Bulbasaur card is card #44 in the 102-card Base Set. The Jungle Set has 64 cards, and the Fossil Set has 62.

Real Card

If a card has a real-world counterpart, it will appear here. If you're familiar with the regular cards, this can help you identify and use the electronic versions.

Hit Points and Evolution

The HP or hits number indicates how much damage a Pokémon can take before it's knocked out. One hit can inflict 10 points of damage. The evolution icon shows whether the Pokémon is a basic, Evol. 1 or Evol. 2 creature. Remember that you can usually play Evol. 1 or Evol. 2 cards only when the proper basic or Evol. 1 card is already in the arena or on the bench.

#1 ●   44/102

BULBASAUR Level 13

HP 40   ◇   Evol. 1 Ivysaur
             Evol. 2 Venusaur

Retreat Cost ✦
Weakness 🔥   **Resistance —**

Leech Seed   🌿🌿   20
Unless all damage from this attack is prevented, you may remove 1 damage counter from Bulbasaur.

BASIC POKéMON   EVOL. 1   EVOL. 2

Attack, Cost and Damage

This section shows the names of the Pokémon's attacks, the energy costs and the damage done to the target. For example, you must place two Grass Energy Cards on Bulbasaur to use its Leech Seed attack, which hits for 20 points of damage. If there are any special instructions or conditions related to an attack, they are shown below the name.

Retreat Cost, Weakness and Resistance

This section shows how much energy to discard when retreating and whether this Pokémon has any particular weakness against or resistance to other Pokémon types. For example, you must discard one Energy Card of any type to return Bulbasaur to the bench, and it has a weakness to Fire-type Pokémon.

Win from ② ⑤ ⑲ ㉑ ㉒ ㉕ ㉚

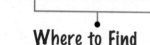

Where to Find

Most of your opponents are numbered in this guide. These numbers are shown on the maps and next to the characters' faces in the strategy section. Defeat the characters listed here to win booster packs that may contain this card.

Game Icon

TYPE ICONS

🌿 GRASS   ⚡ LIGHTNING

🔥 FIRE   ✊ FIGHTING

💧 WATER   👁 PSYCHIC

           ✦ COLORLESS

GRASS POKéMON

#1 ●   44/102

BULBASAUR Level 13

HP 40   Evol. 1 Ivysaur
                   Evol. 2 Venusaur

Retreat Cost

Weakness 🔥   **Resistance** —

Leech Seed   **20**

Unless all damage from this attack is prevented, you may remove 1 damage counter from Bulbasaur.

Win from ② ⑤ ⑲ ㉑ ㉒ ㉕ ㉚

#2 ◆   30/102

IVYSAUR Level 20

HP 60   Basic   Bulbasaur
                   Evol. 2   Venusaur

Retreat Cost

Weakness 🔥   **Resistance** —

Vine Whip   **30**

Poisonpowder   **20**

The Defending Pokémon is now Poisoned.

Win from ② ⑤ ⑲ ㉑ ㉒ ㉕ ㉚

#3 ★   15/102

VENUSAUR Level 67

HP 100   Basic   Bulbasaur
                   Evol. 1   Ivysaur

Retreat Cost

Weakness 🔥   **Resistance** —

Pokémon Power: Energy Trans

As often as you like during your turn (before your attack), you may take 1 🍃 Energy card attached to 1 of your Pokémon and attach it to a different one. This power can't be used if Venusaur is Asleep, Confused, or Paralyzed.

Solarbeam   **60**

Win from ② ⑤ ⑲ ㉑ ㉒ ㉕ ㉚

#10 ●   45/102

CATERPIE Level 13

HP 40   Evol. 1 Metapod
                   Evol. 2 Butterfree

Retreat Cost

Weakness 🔥   **Resistance** —

String Shot   **10**

Flip a coin. If heads, the Defending Pokémon is now Paralyzed.

Win from ② ⑤ ⑲ ㉑ ㉒ ㉕ ㉚

#11 ●   54/102

METAPOD Level 21

HP 70   Basic   Caterpie
                   Evol. 2   Butterfree

Retreat Cost

Weakness 🔥   **Resistance** —

Stiffen

Flip a coin. If heads, prevent all damage done to Metapod during your opponent's next turn. (Any other effects of attacks still happen.)

Stun Spore   **20**

Flip a coin. If heads, the Defending Pokémon is now Paralyzed.

Win from ② ⑤ ⑲ ㉑ ㉒ ㉕ ㉚

BUTTERFREE Level 28

#12 ♦   33/64

HP 70   2↑   Basic   Caterpie   Evol. 1   Metapod

Retreat Cost —

Weakness 🔥   Resistance 👊

Whirlwind   ⭐⭐   **20**
If your opponent has any Benched Pokémon, he or she chooses 1 of them and switches it with the Defending Pokémon. (Do the damage before switching the Pokémon.)

Mega Drain   🍃🍃🍃   **40**
Remove a number of damage counters from Butterfree equal to half the damage done to the Defending Pokémon (after applying Weakness and Resistance) (rounded up to the nearest 10).

Win from ② ⑤ ⑲ ㉑ ㉒ ㉕ ㉚

WEEDLE Level 12

#13 ●   69/102

HP 40   ◇   Evol. 1   Kakuna   Evol. 2   Beedrill

Retreat Cost ⭐

Weakness 🔥   Resistance —

Poison Sting   🍃   **10**
Flip a coin. If heads, the Defending Pokémon is now poisoned.

Win from ② ⑤ ⑲ ㉑ ㉒ ㉕ ㉚

KAKUNA Level 23

#14 ♦   33/102

HP 80   1↑   Basic   Weedle   Evol. 2   Beedrill

Retreat Cost ⭐⭐

Weakness 🔥   Resistance —

Stiffen   ⭐⭐
Flip a coin. If heads, prevent all damage done to Kakuna during your opponent's next turn. (Any other effects of attacks still happen.)

Poisonpowder   🍃🍃   **20**
Flip a coin. If heads, the Defending Pokémon is now poisoned.

Win from ② ⑤ ⑲ ㉑ ㉒ ㉕ ㉚

BEEDRILL Level 32

#15 ★   17/102

HP 80   2↑   Basic   Weedle   Evol. 1   Kakuna

Retreat Cost —

Weakness 🔥   Resistance 👊

Twineedle   ⭐⭐⭐   **30x**
Flip 2 coins. This attack does 30 damage times the number of heads.

Poison Sting   🍃🍃🍃   **40**
Flip a coin. If heads, the Defending Pokémon is now poisoned.

Win from ② ⑤ ⑲ ㉑ ㉒ ㉕ ㉚

EKANS Level 10

#23 ●   46/62

HP 40   ◇   Evol. 1   Arbok

Retreat Cost ⭐

Weakness 👁   Resistance —

Spit Poison   🍃
Flip a coin. If heads, the Defending Pokémon is now poisoned.

Wrap   🍃⭐   **20**
Flip a coin. If heads, the Defending Pokémon is now paralyzed.

Win from ④ ⑫ ⑰ ㉓ ㉔ ㉘

ARBOK Level 27

#24 ♦   31/62

HP 60   1↑   Basic   Ekans

Retreat Cost ⭐⭐

Weakness 👁   Resistance —

Terror Strike   🍃   **10**
Flip a coin. If heads and if your opponent has any Benched Pokémon, he or she chooses 1 of them and switches it with the Defending Pokémon. (Do the damage before switching the Pokémon.)

Poison Fang   🍃🍃⭐   **20**
The Defending Pokémon is now poisoned.

Win from ④ ⑫ ⑰ ㉓ ㉔ ㉘

#29 ● 57/64

NIDORAN♀ Level 13

HP 60 Evol. 1 Nidorina
Evol. 2 Nidoqueen

Retreat Cost
Weakness **Resistance —**

Fury Swipes **10x**

Flip 3 coins. This attack does 10 damage times the number of heads.

Call for Family

Search your deck for a Basic Pokémon named Nidoran ♀ or Nidoran ♂ and put it onto your Bench. Shuffle your deck afterward. (You can't use this attack if your Bench is full.)

Win from ① ⑧ ⑨ ⑪ ⑬ ⑯ ⑱ ⑳ ㉙ ㉜

#30 ♦ 40/64

NIDORINA Level 24

HP 70 Basic Nidoran ♀
Evol. 2 Nidoqueen

Retreat Cost
Weakness **Resistance —**

Supersonic

Flip a coin. If heads, the Defending Pokémon is now confused.

Double Kick **30x**

Flip 2 coins. This attack does 30 damage times the number of heads.

Win from ① ⑧ ⑨ ⑪ ⑬ ⑯ ⑱ ⑳ ㉙ ㉜

#31 ★ 23/64

NIDOQUEEN Level 43

HP 90 Basic Nidoran ♀
Evol. 1 Nidorina

Retreat Cost
Weakness **Resistance —**

Boyfriends **20+**

Does 20 damage plus 20 more damage for each Nidoking you have in play.

Mega Punch **50**

Win from ① ⑧ ⑨ ⑪ ⑬ ⑯ ⑱ ⑳ ㉙ ㉜

#32 ● 55/102

NIDORAN♂ Level 20

HP 40 Evol. 1 Nidorino
Evol. 2 Nidoking

Retreat Cost
Weakness **Resistance —**

Horn Hazard **30**

Flip a coin. If tails, this attack does nothing.

Win from ③ ⑥ ⑦ ⑩ ⑭ ⑮ ㉖ ㉗ ㉛

#33 ♦ 37/102

NIDORINO Level 25

HP 60 Basic Nidoran ♂
Evol. 2 Nidoking

Retreat Cost
Weakness **Resistance —**

Double Kick **30x**

Flip 2 coins. This attack does 30 damage times the number of heads.

Horn Drill  **50**

Win from ③ ⑥ ⑦ ⑩ ⑭ ⑮ ㉖ ㉗ ㉛

#34 ★ 11/102

NIDOKING Level 48

HP 90 Basic Nidoran ♂
Evol. 1 Nidorino

Retreat Cost
Weakness **Resistance —**

Thrash **30+**

Flip a coin. If heads, this attack does 30 damage plus 10 more damage; if tails, this attack does 30 damage and Nidoking does 10 damage to itself.

Toxic **20**

The Defending Pokémon is now poisoned. It now takes 20 poison damage instead of 10 after each player's turn (even if it was already poisoned).

Win from ② ⑤ ⑲ ㉑ ㉒ ㉕ ㉚

ZUBAT Level 10

#41 ●   57/62

HP 40 ◇   Evol. 1 Golbat

Retreat Cost —

Weakness   Resistance

Supersonic ★ ★

Flip a coin. If heads, the Defending Pokémon is now confused.

Leech Life ★ ★   10

Remove a number of damage counters from Zubat equal to the damage done to the Defending Pokémon (after applying Weakness and Resistance). If Zubat has fewer damage counters than that, remove all of them.

Win from ④ ⑫ ⑰ ㉓ ㉔ ㉘

GOLBAT Level 29

#42 ◆   34/62

HP 60 ⬆1   Basic   Zubat

Retreat Cost —

Weakness   Resistance

Wing Attack ★ ★ ★   30

Leech Life 🍃 🍃 ★   20

Remove a number of damage counters from Golbat equal to the damage done to the Defending Pokémon (after applying Weakness and Resistance). If Golbat has fewer damage counters than that, remove all of them.

Win from ④ ⑫ ⑰ ㉓ ㉔ ㉘

ODDISH Level 8

#43 ●   58/64

HP 50 ◇   Evol. 1 Gloom
                   Evol. 2 Vileplume

Retreat Cost ★

Weakness   Resistance —

Stun Spore 🍃   10

Flip a coin. If heads, the Defending Pokémon is now paralyzed.

Sprout 🍃 🍃

Search your deck for a Basic Pokémon named Oddish and put it onto your Bench. Shuffle your deck afterward. (You can't use this attack if your Bench is full.)

Win from ① ⑧ ⑨ ⑪ ⑬ ⑯ ⑱ ⑳ ㉙ ㉜

GLOOM Level 22

#44 ◆   37/64

HP 60 ⬆1   Basic   Oddish
                   Evol. 2 Vileplume

Retreat Cost ★

Weakness   Resistance —

Poisonpowder 🍃

The Defending Pokémon is now poisoned.

Foul Odor 🍃 🍃   20

Both the Defending Pokémon and Gloom are now confused (after doing damage).

Win from ① ⑧ ⑨ ⑪ ⑬ ⑯ ⑱ ⑳ ㉙ ㉜

VILEPLUME Level 35

#45 ★   31/64

HP 80 ⬆2   Basic   Oddish
                   Evol. 1 Gloom

Retreat Cost ★ ★

Weakness   Resistance —

Pokémon Power: Heal

Once during your turn (before your attack), you may flip a coin. If heads, remove 1 damage counter from 1 of your Pokémon. This power can't be used if Vileplume is asleep, confused, or paralyzed.

Petal Dance 🍃 🍃 🍃   40x

Flip 3 coins. This attack does 40 damage times the number of heads. Vileplume is now confused (after doing damage).

Win from ① ⑧ ⑨ ⑪ ⑬ ⑯ ⑱ ⑳ ㉙ ㉜

PARAS Level 8

#46 ●   59/64

HP 40 ◇   Evol. 1 Parasect

Retreat Cost ★

Weakness   Resistance —

Scratch ★ ★   20

Spore 🍃 🍃

The Defending Pokémon is now asleep.

Win from ① ⑧ ⑨ ⑪ ⑬ ⑯ ⑱ ⑳ ㉙ ㉜

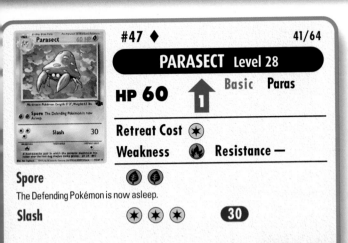

#47 ◆   **41/64**

PARASECT Level 28

HP 60 ↑1 Basic Paras

Retreat Cost ✱

Weakness 🔥 **Resistance** —

Spore 🍃🍃
The Defending Pokémon is now asleep.

Slash ✱✱✱ **30**

Win from ① ⑧ ⑨ ⑪ ⑬ ⑯ ⑱ ⑳ ㉙ ㉜

#48 ●   **63/64**

VENONAT Level 12

HP 40 ◇ Evol. 1 Venomoth

Retreat Cost ✱

Weakness 🔥 **Resistance** —

Stun Spore 🍃 **10**
Flip a coin. If heads, the Defending Pokémon is now paralyzed.

Leech Life 🍃✱ **10**
Remove a number of damage counters from Venonat equal to the damage done to the Defending Pokémon (after applying Weakness and Resistance).

Win from ④ ⑫ ⑰ ㉓ ㉔ ㉘

#49 ★   **29/64**

VENOMOTH Level 28

HP 70 ↑1 Basic Venonat

Retreat Cost —

Weakness 🔥 **Resistance** ✊

Pokémon Power: Shift

Once during your turn (before your attack), you may change the type of Venomoth to the type of any other Pokémon in play other than Colorless. This power can't be used if Venomoth is asleep, confused, or paralyzed.

Venom Powder 🍃🍃 **10**
Flip a coin. If heads, the Defending Pokémon is now confused and poisoned.

Win from ④ ⑫ ⑰ ㉓ ㉔ ㉘

#69 ●   **49/64**

BELLSPROUT Level 11

HP 40 ◇ Evol. 1 Weepinbell
                  Evol. 2 Victreebel

Retreat Cost ✱

Weakness 🔥 **Resistance** —

Vine Whip 🍃 **10**

Call for Family 🍃
Search your deck for a Basic Pokémon named Bellsprout and put it onto your Bench. Shuffle your deck afterward. (You can't use this attack if your Bench is full.)

Win from ② ⑤ ⑲ ㉑ ㉒ ㉕ ㉚

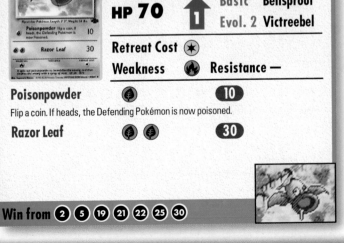

#70 ◆   **48/64**

WEEPINBELL Level 28

HP 70 ↑1 Basic Bellsprout
                  Evol. 2 Victreebel

Retreat Cost ✱

Weakness 🔥 **Resistance** —

Poisonpowder 🍃 **10**
Flip a coin. If heads, the Defending Pokémon is now poisoned.

Razor Leaf 🍃🍃 **30**

Win from ② ⑤ ⑲ ㉑ ㉒ ㉕ ㉚

#71 ★   **30/64**

VICTREEBEL Level 42

HP 80 ↑2 Basic Bellsprout
                  Evol. 1 Weepinbell

Retreat Cost ✱✱

Weakness 🔥 **Resistance** —

Lure 🍃
If your opponent has any Benched Pokémon, choose 1 of them and switch it with his or her Active Pokémon.

Acid 🍃🍃 **20**
Flip a coin. If heads, the Defending Pokémon can't retreat during your opponent's next turn.

Win from ② ⑤ ⑲ ㉑ ㉒ ㉕ ㉚

#88 ●   48/62

GRIMER Level 17

HP 50   Evol. 1   Muk

Retreat Cost ✦

Weakness 👁   **Resistance** —

Nasty Goo   ✦   `10`

Flip a coin. If heads, the Defending Pokémon is now paralyzed.

Minimize   🍃

All damage done by attacks to Grimer during your opponent's next turn is reduced by 20 (after applying Weakness and Resistance).

Win from ④ ⑫ ⑰ ㉓ ㉔ ㉘

#89 ★   28/62

MUK Level 34

HP 70   ⬆1   Basic   Grimer

Retreat Cost ✦ ✦

Weakness 👁   **Resistance** —

Pokémon Power: Toxic Gas

Ignore all Pokémon Powers other than Toxic Gases. This power stops working while Muk is asleep, confused, or paralyzed.

Sludge   🍃 🍃 🍃   `30`

Flip a coin. If heads, the Defending Pokémon is now poisoned.

Win from ④ ⑫ ⑰ ㉓ ㉔ ㉘

#102 ●   52/64

EXEGGCUTE Level 14

HP 50   Evol. 1   Exeggutor

Retreat Cost ✦

Weakness 🔥   **Resistance** —

Hypnosis   👁

The Defending Pokémon is now asleep.

Leech Seed   🍃 🍃   `20`

Unless all damage from this attack is prevented, you may remove 1 damage counter from Exeggcute.

Win from ① ⑧ ⑨ ⑪ ⑬ ⑯ ⑱ ⑳ ㉙ ㉜

#103 ◆   35/64

EXEGGUTOR Level 35

HP 80   ⬆1   Basic   Exeggcute

Retreat Cost ✦ ✦ ✦

Weakness 🔥   **Resistance** —

Teleport   👁

Switch Exeggutor with 1 of your Benched Pokémon.

Big Eggsplosion   ✦   `20x`

Flip a number of coins equal to the number of Energy attached to Exeggutor. This attack does 20 damage times the number of heads.

Win from ① ⑧ ⑨ ⑪ ⑬ ⑯ ⑱ ⑳ ㉙ ㉜

#109 ●   51/102

KOFFING Level 13

HP 50   Evol. 1   Weezing

Retreat Cost ✦

Weakness 👁   **Resistance** —

Foul Gas   🍃 🍃   `10`

Flip a coin. If heads, the Defending Pokémon is now poisoned; if tails, it is now confused.

Win from ④ ⑫ ⑰ ㉓ ㉔ ㉘

#110 ◆   45/62

WEEZING Level 27

HP 60   ⬆1   Basic   Koffing

Retreat Cost ✦

Weakness 👁   **Resistance** —

Smog   🍃 🍃   `20`

Flip a coin. If heads, the Defending Pokémon is now poisoned.

Selfdestruct   🍃 🍃 ✦   `60`

Does 10 damage to each Pokémon on each player's Bench. (Don't apply Weakness and Resistance for Benched Pokémon.) Weezing does 60 damage to itself.

Win from ④ ⑫ ⑰ ㉓ ㉔ ㉘

#114 ● 66/102

TANGELA Level 8

HP 50 ◇

Retreat Cost ✱ ✱
Weakness 🔥 Resistance —

Bind 🌿✱ 20
Flip a coin. If heads, the Defending Pokémon is now paralyzed.

Poisonpowder 🌿🌿🌿 20
The Defending Pokémon is now poisoned.

Win from ④ ⑫ ⑰ ㉓ ㉔ ㉘

#114 ● 66/102

POKéMON
TANGELA

TANGELA Level 12

HP 50 ◇

Retreat Cost ✱ ✱
Weakness 🔥 Resistance —

Stun Spore 🌿 10
Flip a coin. If heads, the Defending Pokémon is now paralyzed.

Poison Whip 🌿🌿✱ 10
The Defending Pokémon is now poisoned.

GAME BOY ONLY

Win from ③ ⑥ ⑦ ⑩ ⑭ ⑮ ㉖ ㉗ ㉛

#123 ★ 26/64

SCYTHER Level 25

HP 70 ◇

Retreat Cost —
Weakness 🔥 Resistance ✊

Swords Dance 🌿
During your next turn, Scyther's Slash attack's base damage is 60 instead of 30.

Slash ✱✱✱ 30

Win from ③ ⑥ ⑦ ⑩ ⑭ ⑮ ㉖ ㉗ ㉛

#127 ★ 25/64

PINSIR Level 24

HP 60 ◇

Retreat Cost ✱
Weakness 🔥 Resistance —

Irongrip 🌿🌿 20
Flip a coin. If heads, the Defending Pokémon is now paralyzed.

Guillotine 🌿🌿🌿✱ 50

Win from ③ ⑥ ⑦ ⑩ ⑭ ⑮ ㉖ ㉗ ㉛

FIRE POKéMON

#4 ● 46/102

CHARMANDER Level 10

HP 50 ◇ Evol. 1 Charmeleon
Evol. 2 Charizard

Retreat Cost ✱
Weakness 💧 Resistance

Scratch ✱ 10

Ember 🔥✱ 30
Discard 1 🔥 Energy card attached to Charmander in order to use this attack.

Win from ③ ⑥ ⑦ ⑩ ⑭ ⑮ ㉖ ㉗ ㉛

CHARMELEON Level 32

HP 80 Basic **Charmander**
Evol. 2 **Charizard**

Retreat Cost ⭐

Weakness 🌊   **Resistance** —

Slash   ⭐ ⭐ ⭐   **30**

Flamethrower   🔥 🔥 ⭐   **50**

Discard 1 🔥 Energy card attached to Charmeleon in order to use this attack.

CHARIZARD Level 76

HP 120 Basic **Charmander**
Evol. 1 **Charmeleon**

Retreat Cost ⭐ ⭐ ⭐

Weakness 🌊   **Resistance** 👊

Pokémon Power: Energy Burn

As often as you like during your turn (before your attack), you may turn all Energy attached to Charizard into 🔥 Energy for the rest of the turn. This power can't be used if Charizard is asleep, confused, or paralyzed.

Fire Spin   🔥 🔥 🔥 🔥   **100**

Discard 2 Energy Cards attached to Charizard in order to use this attack.

VULPIX Level 11

HP 50 ◇ Evol. 1 **Ninetales**

Retreat Cost ⭐

Weakness 💧   **Resistance** —

Confuse Ray   🔥 🔥   **10**

Flip a coin. If heads, the Defending Pokémon is now confused.

NINETALES Level 32

HP 80 Basic **Vulpix**

Retreat Cost ⭐

Weakness 💧   **Resistance** —

Lure   ⭐ ⭐

If your opponent has any Benched Pokémon, choose 1 of them and switch it with the Defending Pokémon.

First Blast   🔥 🔥 🔥 🔥   **80**

Discard 1 🔥 Energy card attached to Ninetales in order to use this attack.

NINETALES Level 35

HP 80 Basic **Vulpix**

Retreat Cost ⭐

Weakness 💧   **Resistance** —

Mix-Up   🔥 🔥

If your opponent has any Basic Pokémon or Evolution cards in his or her hand, your opponent shuffles them into his or her deck. Then, your opponent puts an equal number of Basic Pokémon or Evolution cards chosen at random from his or her deck into his or her hand. Your opponent shuffles his or her deck afterward.

Dancing Embers   🔥 🔥 🔥   **10x**

Flip 8 coins. This attack does 10 damage times the number of heads.

GAME BOY ONLY

GROWLITHE Level 18

HP 60 ◇ Evol. 1 **Arcanine**

Retreat Cost ⭐

Weakness 💧   **Resistance** —

Flare   🔥 ⭐   **20**

#59 ◆   23/102

ARCANINE Level 45

HP 100 **Basic** Growlithe

Retreat Cost ✶ ✶ ✶

Weakness 🔥 Resistance —

Flamethrower 🔥 🔥 ✶ **50**

Discard 1 🔥 Energy card attached to Arcanine in order to use this attack.

Take Down 🔥 🔥 ✶ ✶ **80**

Arcanine does 30 damage to itself.

#77 ●   60/102

PONYTA Level 10

HP 40 ◇ **Evol. 1 Rapidash**

Retreat Cost ✶

Weakness 🔥 Resistance —

Smash Kick ✶ ✶ **20**

Flame Tail 🔥 🔥 **30**

#78 ◆   44/64

RAPIDASH Level 33

HP 70 **Basic** Ponyta

Retreat Cost —

Weakness 🔥 Resistance —

Stomp ✶ ✶ **20+**

Flip a coin. If heads, this attack does 20 damage plus 10 more damage; if tails, this attack does 20 damage.

Agility 🔥 🔥 ✶ **30**

Flip a coin. If heads, during your opponent's next turn, prevent all effects of attacks, including damage, done to Rapidash.

#126 ◆   36/102

MAGMAR Level 24

HP 50 ◇

Retreat Cost ✶ ✶

Weakness 🔥 Resistance —

Fire Punch 🔥 🔥 **30**

Flamethower 🔥 🔥 ✶ **50**

Discard 1 🔥 Energy Card attached to Magmar in order to use this attack.

#126 ◆   39/62

MAGMAR Level 31

HP 70 ◇

Retreat Cost ✶

Weakness 🔥 Resistance —

Attack	Cost	Damage
Smokescreen	🔥	**10**

If the Defending Pokémon tries to attack during your opponent's next turn, your opponent flips a coin. If tails, that attack does nothing.

Smog 🔥 🔥 **20**

Flip a coin. If heads, the Defending Pokémon is now poisoned.

#136 ◆

FLAREON Level 22

HP 60 **Basic** Eevee

Retreat Cost ✶

Weakness 🔥 Resistance —

Bite ✶ ✶ ✶ **30**

Rage ✶ ✶ ✶ **10+**

Does 10 damage plus 10 more damage for each damage counter on Flareon.

GAME BOY ONLY

FLAREON Level 28
#136 ★ 19/64

HP 70   Basic Eevee

Retreat Cost
Weakness   Resistance —

Quick Attack   **10+**

Flip a coin. If heads, this attack does 10 damage plus 20 more damage; if tails, this attack does 10 damage.

Flamethrower **60**

Discard 1 Energy card attached to Flareon in order to use this attack.

Win from  ② ⑤ ⑲ ㉑ ㉒ ㉕ ㉚

MOLTRES Level 35
#146 ★ 27/62

HP 70

Retreat Cost
Weakness — Resistance

Wildfire

You may discard any number of Energy cards attached to Moltres when you use this attack. If you do, discard that many cards from the top of your opponent's deck.

Dive Bomb **80**

Flip a coin. If tails, this attack does nothing.

Win from  ① ⑧ ⑨ ⑪ ⑬ ⑯ ⑱ ⑳ ㉙ ㉜

WATER POKéMON

SQUIRTLE Level 8
#7 ● 63/102

HP 40   Evol. 1 Wartortle
 Evol. 2 Blastoise

Retreat Cost
Weakness   Resistance —

Bubble   **10**

Flip a coin. If heads, the Defending Pokémon is now paralyzed.

Withdraw

Flip a coin. If heads, prevent all damage done to Squirtle during your opponent's next turn. (Any other effects of attacks still happen.)

Win from ② ⑤ ⑲ ㉑ ㉒ ㉕ ㉚

WARTORTLE Level 22
#8 ◆ 42/102

HP 70   Basic Squirtle
 Evol. 2 Blastoise

Retreat Cost
Weakness   Resistance —

Withdraw

Flip a coin. If heads, prevent all damage done to Wartortle during your opponent's next turn. (Any other effects of attacks still happen.)

Bite   **40**

Win from  ② ⑤ ⑲ ㉑ ㉒ ㉕ ㉚

BLASTOISE Level 52
#9 ★ 2/102

HP 100 Basic Squirtle
 Evol. 1 Wartortle

Retreat Cost
Weakness   Resistance —

Pokémon Power: Rain Dance

As often as you like during your turn (before your attack), you may attach 1 Energy Card to 1 of your Pokémon. (This doesn't use up your 1 Energy Card attachment for the turn.) This power can't be used if Blastoise is asleep, confused, or paralyzed.

Hydro Pump **40+**

Does 40 damage plus 10 more damage for each Energy attached to Blastoise but not used to pay for this attack's Energy cost. Extra Energy after the 2nd doesn't count.

Win from  ② ⑤ ⑲ ㉑ ㉒ ㉕ ㉚

PSYDUCK Level 15
#54 ●   53/62

HP 50   Evol. 1 Goldduck

Retreat Cost ✴

Weakness ⚡   Resistance —

Headache 👁
Your opponent can't play Trainer Cards during his or her next turn.

Fury Swipes 🌊   **10x**
Flip 3 coins. This attack does 10 damage times the number of heads.

Win from ④ ⑫ ⑰ ㉓ ㉔ ㉘

GOLDUCK Level 27
#55 ◆   35/62

HP 70 ⬆1   Basic   Psyduck

Retreat Cost ✴

Weakness ⚡   Resistance —

Psyshock 👁   **10**
Flip a coin. If heads, the Defending Pokémon is now paralyzed.

Hyper Beam 🌊🌊✴   **20**
If the Defending Pokémon has any Energy Cards attached to it, choose 1 of them and discard it.

Win from ④ ⑫ ⑰ ㉓ ㉔ ㉘

POLIWAG Level 13
#60 ●   59/102

HP 40   Evol. 1 Poliwhirl / Evol. 2 Poliwrath

Retreat Cost ✴

Weakness 🌿   Resistance —

Water Gun 🌊   **10+**
Does 10 damage plus 10 more damage for each 🌊 Energy attached to Poliwag but not used to pay for this attack's Energy cost. Extra 🌊 Energy after the 2nd don't count.

Win from ④ ⑫ ⑰ ㉓ ㉔ ㉘

POLIWHIRL Level 28
#61 ◆   38/102

HP 60 ⬆1   Basic Poliwag / Evol. 2 Poliwrath

Retreat Cost ✴

Weakness 🌿   Resistance —

Amnesia 🌊🌊
Choose 1 of the Defending Pokémon's attacks. That Pokémon can't use that attack during your opponent's next turn.

Doubleslap 🌊🌊✴   **30x**
Flip 2 coins. This attack does 30 damage times the number of heads.

Win from ④ ⑫ ⑰ ㉓ ㉔ ㉘

POLIWRATH Level 48
#62 ★   13/102

HP 90 ⬆2   Basic Poliwag / Evol. 1 Poliwhirl

Retreat Cost ✴✴✴

Weakness 🌿   Resistance —

Water Gun 🌊🌊✴   **30+**
Does 30 damage plus 10 more damage for each 🌊 Energy attached to Poliwrath but not used to pay for this attack's Energy cost. Extra 🌊 Energy after the 2nd doesn't count.

Whirlpool 🌊🌊✴✴   **40**
If the Defending Pokémon has any Energy Cards attached to it, choose 1 of them and discard it.

Win from ④ ⑫ ⑰ ㉓ ㉔ ㉘

TENTACOOL Level 10
#72 ●   56/62

HP 30   Evol. 1 Tentacruel

Retreat Cost —

Weakness ⚡   Resistance —

Pokémon Power: Cowardice
At any time during your turn (before your attack), you may return Tentacool to your hand. (Discard all cards attached to Tentacool.) This power can't be used the turn you put Tentacool into play or if Tentacool is asleep, confused, or paralyzed.

Acid 🌊   **10**

Win from ④ ⑫ ⑰ ㉓ ㉔ ㉘

 **#73 ◆**   44/62

TENTACRUEL Level 21

HP 60   Basic   Tentacool

Retreat Cost —
Weakness ⚡ Resistance —

Supersonic
Flip a coin. If heads, the Defending Pokémon is now confused.

Jellyfish Sting ◉◉   **10**
The Defending Pokémon is now poisoned.

Win from ④ ⑫ ⑰ ㉓ ㉔ ㉘

 **#86 ◆**   41/102

SEEL Level 12

HP 60   Evol. 1   Dewgong

Retreat Cost ✴
Weakness ⚡ Resistance —

Headbutt ◉   **10**
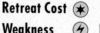

Win from ③ ⑥ ⑦ ⑩ ⑭ ⑮ ㉖ ㉗ ㉛

 #87 ◆   25/102

DEWGONG Level 42

HP 80   Basic   Seel

Retreat Cost ✴ ✴ ✴
Weakness ⚡ Resistance —

Aurora Beam   **50**
Ice Beam   **30**
Flip a coin. If heads, the Defending Pokémon is now paralyzed.

Win from ③ ⑥ ⑦ ⑩ ⑭ ⑮ ㉖ ㉗ ㉛

#90 ●   54/62

SHELLDER Level 8

HP 30   Evol. 1   Cloyster

Retreat Cost ✴
Weakness ⚡ Resistance —

Supersonic
Flip a coin. If heads, the Defending Pokémon is now confused.

Hide in Shell
Flip a coin. If heads, prevent all damage done to Shellder during your opponent's next turn. (Any other effects of attacks still happen.)

Win from ① ⑧ ⑨ ⑪ ⑬ ⑯ ⑱ ⑳ ㉙ ㉜

 #91 ◆   32/62

CLOYSTER Level 25

HP 50   Basic   Shellder

Retreat Cost ✴ ✴
Weakness ⚡ Resistance —

Clamp ◉◉   **30**
Flip a coin. If heads, the Defending Pokémon is now paralyzed. If tails, this attack does nothing (not even damage).

Spike Cannon ◉◉   **30x**
Flip 2 coins. This attack does 30 damage times the number of heads.

Win from ① ⑧ ⑨ ⑪ ⑬ ⑯ ⑱ ⑳ ㉙ ㉜

#98 ●   51/62

KRABBY Level 20

HP 50   Evol. 1   Kingler

Retreat Cost ✴ ✴
Weakness ⚡ Resistance —

Call for Family
Search your deck for a Basic Pokémon named Krabby and put it onto your Bench. Shuffle your deck afterward. (You can't use this attack if your Bench is full.)

Irongrip ◉✴   **20**

Win from ② ⑤ ⑲ ㉑ ㉒ ㉕ ㉚

#99 ◆   38/62

KINGLER Level 27

HP 60   Basic Krabby

Retreat Cost ✹ ✹ ✹
Weakness ⚡ Resistance —

Flail   10x
Does 10 damage times the number of damage counters on Kingler.

Crabhammer   40

Win from ② ⑤ ⑲ ㉑ ㉒ ㉕ ㉚

#116 ●   49/62

HORSEA Level 19

HP 40  Evol. 1 Seadra

Retreat Cost —
Weakness ⚡ Resistance —

Smokescreen   10
If the Defending Pokémon tries to attack during your opponent's next turn, your opponent flips a coin. If tails, that attack does nothing.

Win from ④ ⑫ ⑰ ㉓ ㉔ ㉘

#117 ◆   42/62

SEADRA Level 23

HP 60   Basic Horsea

Retreat Cost ✹
Weakness ⚡ Resistance —

Water Gun   20+
Does 20 damage plus 10 more damage for each ⬢ Energy attached to Seadra but not used to pay for this attack's Energy cost. You can't add more than 20 damage in this way.

Agility   20
Flip a coin. If heads, during your opponent's next turn, prevent all effects of attacks, including damage, done to Seadra.

Win from ④ ⑫ ⑰ ㉓ ㉔ ㉘

#118 ●   53/64

GOLDEEN Level 12

HP 40   Evol. 1 Seaking

Retreat Cost —
Weakness ⚡ Resistance —

Horn Attack   10

Win from ③ ⑥ ⑦ ⑩ ⑭ ⑮ ㉖ ㉗ ㉛

#119 ◆   46/64

SEAKING Level 28

HP 70   Basic Goldeen

Retreat Cost ✹
Weakness ⚡ Resistance —

Horn Attack   10
Waterfall   30

Win from ③ ⑥ ⑦ ⑩ ⑭ ⑮ ㉖ ㉗ ㉛

#120 ●   65/102

STARYU Level 15

HP 40  Evol. 1 Starmie

Retreat Cost ✹
Weakness ⚡ Resistance —

Slap   20

Win from ③ ⑥ ⑦ ⑩ ⑭ ⑮ ㉖ ㉗ ㉛

STARMIE Level 28

#121 ● 64/102

HP 60 Basic Staryu

Retreat Cost

Weakness **Resistance —**

Recover

Discard 1 Energy Card attached to Starmie in order to use this attack. Remove all damage counters from Starmie.

Star Freeze **20**

Flip a coin. If heads, the Defending Pokémon is now paralyzed.

Win from ② ⑤ ⑲ ㉑ ㉒ ㉕ ㉚

MAGIKARP Level 8

#129 ◆ 35/102

HP 30 Evol. 1 Gyarados

Retreat Cost ✱

Weakness **Resistance —**

Tackle ✱ **10**

Flail   **10x**

Does 10 damage times the number of damage counters on Magikarp.

Win from ③ ⑥ ⑦ ⑩ ⑭ ⑮ ㉖ ㉗ ㉛

GYARADOS Level 41

#130 ★ 6/102

HP 100  Basic Magikarp

Retreat Cost ✱ ✱ ✱

Weakness **Resistance**

Dragon Rage **50**

Bubblebeam **40**

Flip a coin. If heads, the Defending Pokémon is now paralyzed.

Win from ③ ⑥ ⑦ ⑩ ⑭ ⑮ ㉖ ㉗ ㉛

LAPRAS Level 31

#131 ★ 25/62

HP 80

Retreat Cost ✱ ✱

Weakness **Resistance —**

Water Gun   **10+**

Does 10 damage plus 10 more damage for each Energy attached to Lapras but not used to pay for this attack's Energy cost. You can't add more than 20 damage in this way.

Confuse Ray **10**

Flip a coin. If heads, the Defending Pokémon is now confused.

Win from ① ⑧ ⑨ ⑪ ⑬ ⑯ ⑱ ⑳ ㉙ ㉜

VAPOREON Level 29

#134 ◆

POKéMON
VAPOREON

HP 60 Basic Eevee

Retreat Cost ✱

Weakness **Resistance —**

Focus Energy ✱

During your next turn, Vaporeon's Bite attack's base damage is doubled.

Bite ✱ ✱ ✱ **30**

Win from ① ⑧ ⑨ ⑪ ⑬ ⑯ ⑱ ⑳ ㉙ ㉜

VAPOREON Level 42

#134 ★ 28/64

HP 80 Basic Eevee

Retreat Cost ✱

Weakness **Resistance —**

Quick Attack ✱ ✱ **10+**

Flip a coin. If heads, this attack does 10 damage plus 20 more damage; if tails, this attack does 10 damage.

Water Gun 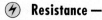 ✱ **30+**

Does 30 damage plus 10 more damage for each Energy attached to Vaporeon but not used to pay for this attack's Energy cost. Extra Energy after the 2nd doesn't count.

Win from ② ⑤ ⑲ ㉑ ㉒ ㉕ ㉚

#138 ● 52/62

OMANYTE Level 19

HP 40

Basic — Myst. Fossil
Evol. 2 — Omastar

Retreat Cost ✶

Weakness **Resistance** —

Pokémon Power: Clairvoyance

Your opponent plays with his or her hand face up. This power stops working while Omanyte is asleep, confused, or paralyzed.

Water Gun **10+**

Does 10 damage plus 10 more damage for each ● Energy attached to Omanyte but not used to pay for this attack's Energy cost. You can't add more than 20 damage in this way.

#139 ◆ 40/62

OMASTAR Level 32

HP 70

Basic — Myst. Fossil
Evol. 1 — Omanyte

Retreat Cost ✶

Weakness **Resistance** —

Water Gun **20+**

Does 20 damage plus 10 more damage for each ● Energy attached to Omastar but not used to pay for this attack's Energy cost. You can't add more than 20 damage in this way.

Spike Cannon **30x**

Flip 2 coins. This attack does 30 damage times the number of heads.

#144 ★ 2/62

ARTICUNO Level 35

HP 70

Retreat Cost ✶ ✶

Weakness **Resistance** ✊

Freeze Dry **30**

Flip a coin. If heads, the Defending Pokémon is now paralyzed.

Blizzard **50**

Flip a coin. If heads, this attack does 10 damage to each of your opponent's Benched Pokémon. If tails, this attack does 10 damage to each of your own Benched Pokémon. (Don't apply Weakness and Resistance for Benched Pokémon.)

LIGHTNING POKéMON

#25 ● 58/102

PIKACHU Level 12

HP 40

Evol. 1 — Raichu

Retreat Cost ✶

Weakness ✊ **Resistance** —

Gnaw ✶ **10**

Thunder Jolt **30**

Flip a coin. If tails, Pikachu does 10 damage to itself.

#25 ● 60/64

PIKACHU Level 14

HP 50

Evol. 1 — Raichu

Retreat Cost ✶

Weakness ✊ **Resistance** —

Spark **20**

If your opponent has any Benched Pokémon, choose 1 of them and this attack does 10 damage to it. (Don't apply Weakness and Resistance for Benched Pokémon.)

RAICHU Level 40

#26 ★   14/102

HP 80   Basic   Pikachu

Retreat Cost

Weakness   **Resistance —**

Agility   **20**

Flip a coin. If heads, during your opponent's next turn, prevent all effects of attacks, including damage, done to Raichu.

Thunder   **60**

Flip a coin. If tails, Raichu does 30 damage to itself.

Win from ③ ⑥ ⑦ ⑩ ⑭ ⑮ ㉖ ㉗ ㉛

RAICHU Level 45

#26 ★   29/62

HP 90   Basic   Pikachu

Retreat Cost

Weakness   **Resistance —**

Gigashock      **30**

Choose 3 of your opponent's Benched Pokémon and this attack does 10 damage to each of them. (Don't apply Weakness and Resistance for Benched Pokémon.) If your opponent has fewer than 3 Benched Pokémon, do the damage to each of them.

Win from ① ⑧ ⑨ ⑪ ⑬ ⑯ ⑱ ⑳ ㉙ ㉜

MAGNEMITE Level 13

#81 ●   53/102

HP 40   ◇   Evol. 1   Magneton

Retreat Cost

Weakness   **Resistance —**

Thunder Wave   **10**

Flip a coin. If heads, the Defending Pokémon is now paralyzed.

Selfdestruct   **40**

Does 10 damage to each Pokémon on each player's Bench. (Don't apply Weakness and Resistance for Benched Pokémon.) Magnemite does 40 damage to itself.

Win from ③ ⑥ ⑦ ⑩ ⑭ ⑮ ㉖ ㉗ ㉛

MAGNEMITE Level 15

#81 ●

HP 40   ◇   Evol. 1   Magneton

Retreat Cost

Weakness   **Resistance —**

Tackle   **10**

Magnetic Storm   ⚡ ★

Remove all Energy Cards attached to all of your Pokémon, then randomly reattach each of them.

Win from ④ ⑫ ⑰ ㉓ ㉔ ㉘

MAGNETON Level 28

#82 ★   9/102

HP 60   Basic   Magnemite

Retreat Cost

Weakness   **Resistance —**

Thunder Wave   **30**

Flip a coin. If heads, the Defending Pokémon is now paralyzed.

Selfdestruct   **80**

Does 20 damage to each Pokémon on each player's Bench. (Don't apply Weakness and Resistance for Benched Pokémon.) Magneton does 80 damage to itself.

Win from ③ ⑥ ⑦ ⑩ ⑭ ⑮ ㉖ ㉗ ㉛

MAGNETON Level 35

#82 ★   11/62

HP 80   Basic   Magnemite

Retreat Cost

Weakness   **Resistance —**

Sonicboom   **20**

Don't apply Weakness and Resistance for this attack. (Any other effects that would happen after applying Weakness and Resistance still happen.)

Selfdestruct   **100**

Does 20 damage to each Pokémon on each player's Bench. (Don't apply Weakness and Resistance for Benched Pokémon.) Magneton does 100 damage to itself.

Win from ④ ⑫ ⑰ ㉓ ㉔ ㉘

VOLTORB Level 10

#100 ● 67/102

VOLTORB Level 10

HP 40 ◇ **Evol. 1** Electrode

Retreat Cost ✦
Weakness ✊ Resistance —

Tackle ✦ **10**

Win from ① ⑧ ⑨ ⑪ ⑬ ⑯ ⑱ ⑳ ㉙ ㉜

ELECTRODE Level 35

POKéMON
ELECTRODE

#101 ★

ELECTRODE Level 35

HP 70 ⬆① **Basic** Voltorb

Retreat Cost ✦
Weakness ✊ Resistance —

Sonicboom ⚡⚡ **30**

Don't apply Weakness and Resistance for this attack. (Any other effects that would happen after applying Weakness and Resistance still happen.)

Energy Spike ⚡⚡⚡

Search your deck for a basic Energy Card and attach it to 1 of your Pokémon. Shuffle your deck afterward.

GAME BOY ONLY

Win from ④ ⑫ ⑰ ㉓ ㉔ ㉘

ELECTRODE Level 42

#101 ★ 18/64

ELECTRODE Level 42

HP 90 ⬆① **Basic** Voltorb

Retreat Cost ✦
Weakness ✊ Resistance —

Tackle ✦✦ **20**

Chain Lightning ⚡⚡⚡ **20**

If the Defending Pokémon isn't Colorless, this attack does 10 damage to each Benched Pokémon of the same type as the Defending Pokémon (including your own).

Win from ① ⑧ ⑨ ⑪ ⑬ ⑯ ⑱ ⑳ ㉙ ㉜

ELECTABUZZ Level 35

#125 ★ 20/102

ELECTABUZZ Level 35

HP 70 ◇

Retreat Cost ✦✦
Weakness ✊ Resistance —

Thundershock ⚡ **10**

Flip a coin. If heads, the Defending Pokémon is now paralyzed.

Thunderpunch ⚡✦ **30+**

Flip a coin. If heads, this attack does 30 damage plus 10 more damage; if tails, this attack does 30 damage and Electabuzz does 10 damage to itself.

Win from ③ ⑥ ⑦ ⑩ ⑭ ⑮ ㉖ ㉗ ㉛

JOLTEON Level 24

POKéMON
JOLTEON

#135 ◆

JOLTEON Level 24

HP 60 ⬆① **Basic** Eevee

Retreat Cost ✦
Weakness ✊ Resistance —

Double Kick ✦✦ **20x**

Flip 2 coins. This attack does 20 damage times the number of heads.

Stun Needle ✦✦✦✦ **30**

Flip a coin. If heads, the Defending Pokémon is now paralyzed.

GAME BOY ONLY

Win from ① ⑧ ⑨ ⑪ ⑬ ⑯ ⑱ ⑳ ㉙ ㉜

JOLTEON Level 29

#135 ★ 20/64

JOLTEON Level 29

HP 70 ⬆① **Basic** Eevee

Retreat Cost ✦
Weakness ✊ Resistance —

Quick Attack ✦✦ **10+**

Flip a coin. If heads, this attack does 10 damage plus 20 more damage; if tails, this attack does 10 damage.

Pin Missile ⚡⚡✦ **20x**

Flip 4 coins. This attack does 20 damage times the number of heads.

Win from ② ⑤ ⑲ ㉑ ㉒ ㉕ ㉚

#145 ★   30/62

ZAPDOS Level 40

HP 80

Retreat Cost ✴ ✴

Weakness — **Resistance** ✊

Thunderstorm ⚡ ⚡ ⚡ ⚡ **40**

For each of your opponent's Benched Pokémon, flip a coin. If heads, this attack does 20 damage to that Pokémon. (Don't apply Weakness and Resistance for Benched Pokémon.) Then, Zapdos does 10 damage times the number of tails to itself.

Win from ① ⑧ ⑨ ⑪ ⑬ ⑯ ⑱ ⑳ ㉙ ㉜

#145 ★   16/102

ZAPDOS Level 64

HP 90

Retreat Cost ✴ ✴ ✴

Weakness — **Resistance** ✊

Attack	Cost	Damage
Thunder	⚡ ⚡ ⚡ ✴	**60**

Flip a coin. If tails, Zapdos does 30 damage to itself.

| **Thunderbolt** | ⚡ ⚡ ⚡ ⚡ | **100** |

Discard all Energy Cards attached to Zapdos in order to use this attack.

Win from ③ ⑥ ⑦ ⑩ ⑭ ⑮ ㉖ ㉗ ㉛

PSYCHIC POKéMON

#63 ●   43/102

ABRA Level 10

HP 30   Evol. 1 Kadabra
                                Evol. 2 Alakazam

Retreat Cost —

Weakness 👁 **Resistance** —

Psyshock 👁 **10**

Flip a coin. If heads, the Defending Pokémon is now paralyzed.

Win from ③ ⑥ ⑦ ⑩ ⑭ ⑮ ㉖ ㉗ ㉛

#64 ◆   32/102

KADABRA Level 38

HP 60   Basic Abra
                              Evol. 2 Alakazam

Retreat Cost ✴ ✴ ✴

Weakness 👁 **Resistance** —

Recover 👁 👁

Discard 1 👁 Energy Card attached to Kadabra in order to use this attack. Remove all damage counters from Kadabra.

Super Psy 👁 👁 ✴ **50**

Win from ③ ⑥ ⑦ ⑩ ⑭ ⑮ ㉖ ㉗ ㉛

#65 ★   1/102

ALAKAZAM Level 42

HP 80   Basic Abra
                              Evol. 1 Kadabra

Retreat Cost ✴ ✴ ✴

Weakness 👁 **Resistance** —

Pokémon Power: Damage Swap

As often as you like during your turn (before your attack), you may move 1 damage counter from 1 of your Pokémon to another as long as you don't Knock Out that Pokémon. This power can't be used if Alakazam is asleep, confused, or paralyzed.

Confuse Ray 👁 👁 👁 **30**

Flip a coin. If heads, the Defending Pokémon is now confused.

Win from ① ⑧ ⑨ ⑪ ⑬ ⑯ ⑱ ⑳ ㉙ ㉜

#79 ●   55/62

SLOWPOKE Level 18

HP 50   ◇   Evol. 1   Slowbro

Retreat Cost ★

Weakness ◎   **Resistance** —

Spacing Out ★

Flip a coin. If heads, remove a damage counter from Slowpoke. This attack can't be used if Slowpoke has no damage counters on it.

Scavenge ◎ ◎

Discard 1 ◎ Energy Card attached to Slowpoke in order to use this attack. Put a Trainer Card from your discard pile into your hand.

Win from ④ ⑫ ⑰ ㉓ ㉔ ㉘

#80 ◆   43/62

SLOWBRO Level 26

HP 60   ⬆   Basic   Slowpoke

Retreat Cost ★

Weakness ◎   **Resistance** —

Pokémon Power: Strange Behavior

As often as you like during your turn (before your attack), you may move 1 damage counter from 1 of your Pokémon to Slowbro as long as you don't Knock Out Slowbro. This power can't be used if Slowbro is asleep, confused, or paralyzed.

Psyshock ◎ ◎   20

Flip a coin. If heads, the Defending Pokémon is now Paralyzed.

Win from ④ ⑫ ⑰ ㉓ ㉔ ㉘

#92 ●   50/102

GASTLY Level 8

HP 30   ◇   Evol. 1   Haunter
                   Evol. 2   Gengar

Retreat Cost —

Weakness —   **Resistance** ✊

Sleeping Gas ◎

Flip a coin. If heads, the Defending Pokémon is now asleep.

Destiny Bond ◎ ★

Discard 1 ◎ Energy card attached to Gastly in order to use this attack. If a Pokémon Knocks Out Gastly during your opponent's next turn, Knock Out that Pokémon.

Win from ② ⑤ ⑲ ㉑ ㉒ ㉕ ㉚

#92 ◆   33/62

GASTLY Level 17

HP 50   ◇   Evol. 1   Haunter
                   Evol. 2   Gengar

Retreat Cost —

Weakness —   **Resistance** ✊

Lick ◎   10

Flip a coin. If heads, the Defending Pokémon is now paralyzed.

Energy Conversion ◎ ◎

Put up to 2 Energy Cards from your discard pile into your hand. Gastly does 10 damage to itself.

Win from ④ ⑫ ⑰ ㉓ ㉔ ㉘

#93 ★   21/62

HAUNTER Level 17

HP 50   ⬆   Basic   Gastly
                   Evol. 2   Gengar

Retreat Cost —

Weakness —   **Resistance** ✊

Pokémon Power: Transparency

Whenever an attack does anything to Haunter, flip a coin. If heads, prevent all effects of that attack, including damage, done to Haunter. This power stops working while Haunter is asleep, confused, or paralyzed.

Nightmare ◎ ★   10

The Defending Pokémon is now asleep.

Win from ④ ⑫ ⑰ ㉓ ㉔ ㉘

#93 ◆   29/102

HAUNTER Level 22

HP 60   ⬆   Basic   Gastly
                   Evol. 2   Gengar

Retreat Cost ★

Weakness —   **Resistance** ✊

Hypnosis ◎

The Defending Pokémon is now asleep.

Dream Eater ◎ ◎   50

You can't use this attack unless the Defending Pokémon is asleep.

Win from ② ⑤ ⑲ ㉑ ㉒ ㉕ ㉚

#94 ★　　　　　　　　　　20/62

GENGAR Level 38

HP 80 　Basic　Gastly
　　　　　　　　　Evol. 1　Haunter

Retreat Cost

Weakness —　　Resistance

Pokémon Power: Curse

Once during your turn (before your attack), you may move 1 damage counter from 1 of your opponent's Pokémon to another (even if it would Knock Out the other Pokémon). This power can't be used if Gengar is asleep, confused, or paralyzed.

Dark Mind   　**30**

If your opponent has any Benched Pokémon, choose 1 of them and this attack does 10 damage to it. (Don't apply Weakness and Resistance for Benched Pokémon.)

Win from ② ⑤ ⑲ ㉑ ㉒ ㉕ ㉚

#96 ●　　　　　　　　　　49/102

DROWZEE Level 12

HP 50 　Evol. 1　Hypno

Retreat Cost

Weakness 　Resistance —

Pound 　**10**

Confuse Ray 　**10**

Flip a coin. If heads, the Defending Pokémon is now confused.

Win from ① ⑧ ⑨ ⑪ ⑬ ⑯ ⑱ ⑳ ㉙ ㉜

#97 ★　　　　　　　　　　23/62

HYPNO Level 36

HP 90 　Basic　Drowzee

Retreat Cost

Weakness 　Resistance —

Prophecy

Look at up to 3 cards from the top of either player's deck and rearrange them as you like.

Dark Mind 　**30**

If your opponent has any Benched Pokémon, choose 1 of them and this attack does 10 damage to it. (Don't apply Weakness and Resistance for Benched Pokémon.)

Win from ④ ⑫ ⑰ ㉓ ㉔ ㉘

#122 ★　　　　　　　　　　22/64

MR. MIME Level 28

HP 40

Retreat Cost

Weakness 　Resistance —

Pokémon Power: Invisible Wall

Whenever an attack (including your own) does 30 or more damage to Mr. Mime (after applying Weakness and Resistance), prevent that damage. (Any other effects of attacks still happen.) This power can't be used if Mr. Mime is asleep, confused, or paralyzed.

Meditate 　**10+**

Does 10 damage plus 10 more damage for each damage counter on the Defending Pokémon.

Win from ④ ⑫ ⑰ ㉓ ㉔ ㉘

#124 ◆　　　　　　　　　　31/102

JYNX Level 23

HP 70

Retreat Cost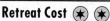

Weakness 　Resistance —

Doubleslap 　**10x**

Flip 2 coins. This attack does 10 damage times the number of heads.

Meditate 　**20+**

Does 20 damage plus 10 more damage for each damage counter on the Defending Pokémon.

Win from ② ⑤ ⑲ ㉑ ㉒ ㉕ ㉚

#150 ★　　　　　　　　　　10/102

MEWTWO Level 53

HP 60

Retreat Cost

Weakness 　Resistance —

Psychic 　**10+**

Does 10 damage plus 10 more damage for each Energy Card attached to the Defending Pokémon.

Barrier

Discard 1 Energy Card attached to Mewtwo in order to use this attack. During your opponent's next turn, prevent all effects of attacks, including damage, done to Mewtwo.

Win from ④ ⑫ ⑰ ㉓ ㉔ ㉘

#151 ◆

MEW Level 23

HP 50

Retreat Cost ★

Weakness 👁 **Resistance** —

Psywave 👁 **10x**

Does 10 damage times the number of Energy Cards attached to the defending Pokémon.

Devolution Beam 👁 👁

Choose an evolved Pokémon (your own or your opponent's). Return the highest Stage Evolution Card on that Pokémon to its player's hand. That Pokémon is no longer asleep, confused, paralyzed, poisoned or anything else that might be the result of an attack (just as if you had evolved it).

Win from 1 8 9 11 13 16 18 20 29 32

FIGHTING POKéMON

#27 ● 62/102

SANDSHREW Level 12

HP 40 **Evol. 1** Sandslash

Retreat Cost ★

Weakness 🍃 **Resistance** ⚡

Sand-Attack **10**

If the Defending Pokémon tries to attack during your opponent's next turn, your opponent flips a coin. If tails, that attack does nothing.

Win from 2 5 19 21 22 25 30

#28 ◆ 41/62

SANDSLASH Level 33

HP 70 **Basic** Sandshrew

Retreat Cost ★

Weakness 🍃 **Resistance** ⚡

Slash ★ ★ **20**

Fury Swipes  **20x**

Flip 3 coins. This attack does 20 damage times the number of heads.

Win from 2 5 19 21 22 25 30

#50 ● 47/102

DIGLETT Level 8

HP 30 **Evol. 1** Dugtrio

Retreat Cost —

Weakness 🍃 **Resistance** ⚡

Dig **10**

Mud Slap   **30**

Win from 3 6 7 10 14 15 26 27 31

#51 ★ 19/102

DUGTRIO Level 36

HP 70 **Basic** Diglett

Retreat Cost ★ ★

Weakness 🍃 **Resistance** ⚡

Slash   **40**

Earthquake 👊 👊 👊 👊 **70**

Does 10 damage to each of your own Benched Pokémon. (Don't apply Weakness and Resistance for Benched Pokémon.)

Win from 3 6 7 10 14 15 26 27 31

#56 ● 55/64

MANKEY Level 7

HP 30 Evol. 1 Primeape

Retreat Cost —

Weakness Resistance —

Pokémon Power: Peek

Once during your turn (before your attack), you may look at one of the following: the top card of either player's deck, a random card from your opponent's hand, or one of either player's Prizes. This power can't be used if Mankey is asleep, confused, or paralyzed.

Scratch **10**

Win from ① ⑧ ⑨ ⑪ ⑬ ⑯ ⑱ ⑳ ㉙ ㉜

#57 ◆ 43/64

PRIMEAPE Level 35

HP 70 Basic Mankey

Retreat Cost

Weakness Resistance —

Fury Swipes **20x**

Flip 3 coins. This attack does 20 damage times the number of heads.

Tantrum **50**

Flip a coin. If tails, Primeape is now confused (after doing damage).

Win from ① ⑧ ⑨ ⑪ ⑬ ⑯ ⑱ ⑳ ㉙ ㉜

#66 ● 52/102

MACHOP Level 20

HP 50 Evol. 1 Machoke

Evol. 2 Machamp

Retreat Cost

Weakness  Resistance —

Low Kick **20**

Win from ③ ⑥ ⑦ ⑩ ⑭ ⑮ ㉖ ㉗ ㉛

#67 ◆ 34/102

MACHOKE Level 40

HP 80 Basic Machop

Evol. 2 Machamp

Retreat Cost

Weakness Resistance —

Karate Chop **50-**

Does 50 damage minus 10 damage for each damage counter on Machoke.

Submission **60**

Machoke does 20 damage to itself.

Win from ② ⑤ ⑲ ㉑ ㉒ ㉕ ㉚

#68 ★ 8/102

MACHAMP Level 67

HP 100 Basic Machop

Evol. 1 Machoke

Retreat Cost

Weakness Resistance —

Pokémon Power: Strikes Back

Whenever your opponent's attack damages Machamp (even if Machamp is Knocked Out), this power does 10 damage to the attacking Pokémon. (Don't apply Weakness and Resistance.) This power can't be used if Machamp is already asleep, confused, or paralyzed when your opponent attacks.

Seismic Toss **60**

Win from ② ⑤ ⑲ ㉑ ㉒ ㉕ ㉚

#74 ● 47/62

GEODUDE Level 16

HP 50 Evol. 1 Graveler

Evol. 2 Golem

Retreat Cost

Weakness Resistance —

Stone Barrage **10x**

Flip a coin until you get tails. This attack does 10 damage times the number of heads.

Win from ② ⑤ ⑲ ㉑ ㉒ ㉕ ㉚

GRAVELER Level 29

#75 ♦   37/62

HP 60 1   Basic   Geodude
         Evol. 2   Golem

Retreat Cost
Weakness Resistance —

Harden

During your opponent's next turn, whenever 30 or less damage is done to Graveler (after applying Weakness and Resistance), prevent that damage. (Any other effects of attacks still happen.)

Rock Throw **40**

Win from

GOLEM Level 36

#76 ♦   36/62

HP 80 2   Basic   Geodude
         Evol. 1   Graveler

Retreat Cost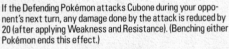
Weakness Resistance —

Avalanche **60**

Selfdestruct **100**

Does 20 damage to each Pokémon on each player's Bench. (Don't apply Weakness and Resistance for Benched Pokémon.) Golem does 100 damage to itself.

Win from

ONIX Level 12

#95 ●   56/102

HP 90 ◇

Retreat Cost
Weakness Resistance —

Rock Throw **10**

Harden

During your opponent's next turn, whenever 30 or less damage is done to Onix (after applying Weakness and Resistance), prevent that damage. (Any other effects of attacks still happen.)

Win from

CUBONE Level 13

#104 ●   50/64

HP 40 ◇   Evol. 1   Marowak

Retreat Cost
Weakness Resistance

Snivel

If the Defending Pokémon attacks Cubone during your opponent's next turn, any damage done by the attack is reduced by 20 (after applying Weakness and Resistance). (Benching either Pokémon ends this effect.)

Rage **10+**

Does 10 damage plus 10 more damage for each damage counter on Cubone.

Win from

MAROWAK Level 26

#105 ♦   39/64

HP 60 1   Basic   Cubone

Retreat Cost
Weakness Resistance

Bonemerang **30x**

Flip 2 coins. This attack does 30 damage times the number of heads.

Call for Friend

Search your deck for a Basic Pokémon card and put it onto your Bench. Shuffle your deck afterward. (You can't use this attack if your Bench is full.)

Win from

MAROWAK Level 32

#105 ♦

HP 70 1   Basic   Cubone

Retreat Cost
Weakness Resistance

Bone Attack **10**

Flip a coin. If heads, the Defending Pokémon can't attack during your opponent's next turn.

Wail

Each player fills his or her Bench with Basic Pokémon chosen at random from his or her deck. If a player has fewer Basic Pokémon than that in his or deck, he or she chooses all of them. Each player shuffles his or her deck afterward.

Win from

GAME
BOY
ONLY

#106 ⭐ HITMONLEE Level 30 22/62

HP 60 ◇

Retreat Cost ⭐
Weakness 👁 Resistance —

Stretch Kick ✊✊
If your opponent has any Benched Pokémon, choose 1 of them and this attack does 20 damage to it. (Don't apply Weakness and Resistance for Benched Pokémon.)

High Jump Kick ✊✊✊ **50**

#107 ⭐ HITMONCHAN Level 33 7/102

HP 70 ◇

Retreat Cost ⭐⭐
Weakness 👁 Resistance —

Jab ✊ **20**

Special Punch ✊✊⭐ **40**

#111 ● RHYHORN Level 18 61/64

HP 70 ◇ Evol. 1 Rhydon

Retreat Cost ⭐⭐⭐
Weakness 🌱 Resistance ⚡

Leer ⭐
Flip a coin. If heads, the Defending Pokémon can't attack Rhyhorn during your opponent's next turn. (Benching either Pokémon ends this effect.)

Horn Attack ✊⭐⭐ **30**

#112 ◆ RHYDON Level 48 45/64

HP 100 ⬆1 Basic Rhyhorn

Retreat Cost ⭐⭐⭐
Weakness 🌱 Resistance ⚡

Horn Attack ✊⭐⭐ **30**

Ram ✊✊✊✊ **50**
Rhydon does 20 damage to itself. If your opponent has any Benched Pokémon, he or she chooses 1 of them and switches it with the Defending Pokémon.(Do the damage before switching the Pokémon. Switch the Pokémon even if Rhydon is Knocked Out.)

#140 ● KABUTO Level 9 50/62

HP 30 ⬆1 Basic Myst. Fossil
  Evol. 2 Kabutops

Retreat Cost ⭐
Weakness 🌱 Resistance —

Pokémon Power: Kabuto Armor
Whenever an attack (even your own) does damage to Kabuto (after applying Weakness and Resistance), that attack only does half the damage to Kabuto (rounded down to the nearest 10). (Any other effects of attacks still happen.) This power stops working while Kabuto is asleep, confused, or paralyzed.

Scratch ⭐ **10**

#141 ⭐ KABUTOPS Level 30 24/62

HP 60 ⬆2 Basic Myst. Fossil
  Evol. 1 Kabuto

Retreat Cost ⭐
Weakness 🌱 Resistance —

Sharp Sickle ✊✊ **30**

Absorb ✊✊✊✊ **40**
Remove a number of damage counters from Kabutops equal to half the damage done to the Defending Pokémon (after applying Weakness and Resistance) (rounded up to the nearest 10). If Kabutops has fewer damage counters than that, remove all of them.

#142 ★   16/62

AERODACTYL Level 28

HP 60   Basic   Myst. Fossil

Retreat Cost ✦ ✦

Weakness   **Resistance**

Pokémon Power: Prehistoric Power

No more Evolution cards can be played. This power stops working while Aerodactyl is asleep, confused, or paralyzed.

Wing Attack   ✦ ✦ ✦   **30**

Win from ① ⑧ ⑨ ⑪ ⑬ ⑯ ⑱ ⑳ ㉙ ㉜

COLORLESS POKéMON

#16 ●   57/102

PIDGEY Level 8

HP 40   Evol. 1   Pidgeotto
                  Evol. 2   Pidgeot

Retreat Cost ✦

Weakness   **Resistance**

Whirlwind   ✦ ✦   **10**

If your opponent has any Benched Pokémon, he or she chooses 1 of them and switches it with the Defending Pokémon. (Do the damage before switching the Pokémon.)

Win from ② ⑤ ⑲ ㉑ ㉒ ㉕ ㉚

#17 ★   22/102

PIDGEOTTO Level 36

HP 60   Basic   Pidgey
                  Evol. 2   Pidgeot

Retreat Cost ✦

Weakness   **Resistance**

Whirlwind   ✦ ✦   **20**

If your opponent has any Benched Pokémon, he or she chooses 1 of them and switches it with the Defending Pokémon. (Do the damage before switching the Pokémon.)

Mirror Move   ✦ ✦ ✦

If Pidgeotto was attacked last turn, do the final result of that attack on Pidgeotto to the Defending Pokémon.

Win from ② ⑤ ⑲ ㉑ ㉒ ㉕ ㉚

#18 ★

PIDGEOT Level 38

HP 80   Basic   Pidgey
                  Evol. 1   Pidgeotto

Retreat Cost ✦

Weakness   **Resistance**

Slicing Wind   ✦ ✦ ✦

Does 30 damage to 1 of your opponent's Pokémon chosen at random. Don't apply Weakness and Resistance for this attack. (Any other effects that would happen after applying Weakness and Resistance still happen.)

Gale   ✦ ✦ ✦ ✦   **20**

Switch Pidgeot with 1 of your Benched Pokémon chosen at random. If your opponent has any Benched Pokémon, switch the Defending Pokémon with 1 of them chosen at random. (Do the damage before switching the Pokémon.)

GAME BOY ONLY

Win from ④ ⑫ ⑰ ㉓ ㉔ ㉘

#18 ★   24/64

PIDGEOT Level 40

HP 80   Basic   Pidgey
                  Evol. 1   Pidgeotto

Retreat Cost —

Weakness   **Resistance**

Wing Attack   ✦ ✦   **20**

Hurricane   ✦ ✦ ✦   **30**

Unless this attack Knocks Out the Defending Pokémon, return the Defending Pokémon and all cards attached to it to your opponent's hand.

Win from ② ⑤ ⑲ ㉑ ㉒ ㉕ ㉚

#19 ● 61/102

RATTATA Level 9

HP 30 Evol. 1 Raticate

Retreat Cost —

Weakness Resistance

Bite ★ 20

Win from ❸ ❻ ❼ ❿ ⓮ ⓯ ㉖ ㉗ ㉛

#20 ◆ 40/102

RATICATE Level 41

HP 60 Basic Rattata

Retreat Cost

Weakness Resistance

Bite ★ 20

Super Fang ★ ★ ★

Does damage to the Defending Pokémon equal to half the
Defending Pokémon's remaining HP (rounded up to the nearest 10).

Win from ❸ ❻ ❼ ❿ ⓮ ⓯ ㉖ ㉗ ㉛

#21 ● 62/64

SPEAROW Level 13

HP 50 Evol. 1 Fearow

Retreat Cost —

Weakness Resistance

Peck ★ 10

Mirror Move ★ ★ ★

If Spearow was attacked last turn, do the final result of that
attack on Spearow to the Defending Pokémon.

Win from ❹ ⓬ ⓱ ㉓ ㉔ ㉘

#22 ◆ 36/64

FEAROW Level 27

HP 70 Basic Spearow

Retreat Cost —

Weakness Resistance

Agility ★ ★ ★ 20

Flip a coin. If heads, during your opponent's next turn, prevent all effects of attacks,
including damage, done to Fearow.

Drill Peck ★ ★ ★ ★ 40

Win from ❹ ⓬ ⓱ ㉓ ㉔ ㉘

#35 ★ 5/102

CLEFAIRY Level 14

HP 40 Evol. 1 Clefable

Retreat Cost ★

Weakness Resistance

Sing ★

Flip a coin. If heads, the Defending Pokémon is now asleep.

Metronome ★ ★ ★

Choose 1 of the Defending Pokémon's attacks. Metronome
copies that attack except for its Energy costs. (No matter
what type the Defending Pokémon is, Clefairy's type is still
Colorless.)

Win from ❶ ❽ ❾ ⓫ ⓭ ⓰ ⓲ ⑳ ㉙ ㉜

#36 ★ 17/64

CLEFABLE Level 34

HP 70 Basic Clefairy

Retreat Cost ★ ★

Weakness Resistance

Metronome ★

Choose 1 of the Defending Pokémon's attacks. Metronome copies that attack except
for its Energy costs. (No matter what type the Defending Pokémon is, Clefable's type
is still Colorless.)

Minimize ★ ★

All damage done by attacks to Clefable during your opponent's next
turn is reduced by 20 (after applying Weakness and Resistance).

Win from ❹ ⓬ ⓱ ㉓ ㉔ ㉘

JIGGLYPUFF Level 13
#39 ●

HP 50 ◇ Evol. 1 Wigglytuff

Retreat Cost ★

Weakness ✊ Resistance 👁

Friendship Song ★
Flip a coin. If heads, put a Basic Pokémon card chosen at random from your deck onto your Bench. (You can't use this attack if your Bench is full.)

Expand ★ ★ 10
All damage done to Jigglypuff during your opponent's next turn is reduced by 10 (after applying Weakness and Resistance).

GAME BOY ONLY

Win from ② ⑤ ⑲ ㉑ ㉒ ㉕ ㉚

JIGGLYPUFF Level 14
#39 ● 54/64

HP 60 ◇ Evol. 1 Wigglytuff

Retreat Cost ★

Weakness ✊ Resistance 👁

Lullaby ★
The Defending Pokémon is now asleep.

Pound ★ ★ 20

Win from ③ ⑥ ⑦ ⑩ ⑭ ⑮ ㉖ ㉗ ㉛

WIGGLYTUFF Level 36
#40 ★ 32/64

HP 80 ⬆1 Basic Jigglypuff

Retreat Cost ★ ★

Weakness ✊ Resistance 👁

Lullaby ★
The Defending Pokémon is now asleep.

Do the Wave ★ ★ ★ 10+
Does 10 damage plus 10 more damage for each of your Benched Pokémon.

Win from ③ ⑥ ⑦ ⑩ ⑭ ⑮ ㉖ ㉗ ㉛

MEOWTH Level 14
#52 ●

HP 50 ◇ Evol. 1 Persian

Retreat Cost ★

Weakness ✊ Resistance 👁

Cat Punch ★ ★
Does 20 damage to 1 of your opponent's Pokémon chosen at random. Don't apply Weakness and Resistance for this attack. (Any other effects that would happen after applying Weakness and Resistance still happen.)

GAME BOY ONLY

Win from ③ ⑥ ⑦ ⑩ ⑭ ⑮ ㉖ ㉗ ㉛

MEOWTH Level 15
#52 ● 56/64

HP 50 ◇ Evol. 1 Persian

Retreat Cost ★

Weakness ✊ Resistance 👁

Pay Day ★ ★ 10
Flip a coin. If heads, draw a card.

Win from ① ⑧ ⑨ ⑪ ⑬ ⑯ ⑱ ⑳ ㉙ ㉜

PERSIAN Level 25
#53 ◆ 42/64

HP 70 ⬆1 Basic Meowth

Retreat Cost —

Weakness ✊ Resistance 👁

Scratch ★ ★ 20

Pounce ★ ★ ★ 30
If the Defending Pokémon attacks Persian during your opponent's next turn, any damage done by the attack is reduced by 10 (after applying Weakness and Resistance). (Benching either Pokémon ends this effect.)

Win from ① ⑧ ⑨ ⑪ ⑬ ⑯ ⑱ ⑳ ㉙ ㉜

#83 ♦   27 /102

FARFETCH'D Level 20

HP 50 ◇

Retreat Cost ★

Weakness ⚡   Resistance ✊

Leek Slap   ★   30

Flip a coin. If tails, this attack does nothing. Either way, you can't use this attack again as long as Farfetch'd stays in play (even putting Farfetch'd on the Bench won't let you use it again).

Pot Smash   ★ ★ ★   30

Win from ① ⑧ ⑨ ⑪ ⑬ ⑯ ⑱ ⑳ ㉙ ㉜

#84 ●   48/102

DODUO Level 10

HP 50 ◇   Evol. 1   Dodrio

Retreat Cost —

Weakness ⚡   Resistance ✊

Fury Attack   ★   10x

Flip 2 coins. This attack does 10 damage times the number of heads.

Win from ④ ⑫ ⑰ ㉓ ㉔ ㉘

#85 ♦   34/64

DODRIO Level 28

HP 70 ⬆   Basic   Doduo

Retreat Cost —

Weakness ⚡   Resistance ✊

Pokémon Power: Retreat Aid

As long as Dodrio is Benched, pay ★ less to retreat your Active Pokémon.

Rage   ★ ★ ★   10+

Does 10 damage plus 10 more damage for each damage counter on Dodrio.

Win from ④ ⑫ ⑰ ㉓ ㉔ ㉘

#108 ♦      38/64

LICKITUNG Level 26

HP 90 ◇

Retreat Cost ★ ★ ★

Weakness ✊   Resistance ◎

Tongue Wrap   ★   10

Flip a coin. If heads, the Defending Pokémon is now paralyzed.

Supersonic   ★ ★

Flip a coin. If heads, the Defending Pokémon is now confused.

Win from ① ⑧ ⑨ ⑪ ⑬ ⑯ ⑱ ⑳ ㉙ ㉜

#113 ★   3/102

CHANSEY Level 55

HP 120 ◇

Retreat Cost ★

Weakness ✊   Resistance ◎

Scrunch   ★ ★

Flip a coin. If heads, prevent all damage done to Chansey during your opponent's next turn. (Any other effects of attacks still happen.)

Double-edge   ★ ★ ★ ★   80

Chansey does 80 damage to itself.

Win from ③ ⑥ ⑦ ⑩ ⑭ ⑮ ㉖ ㉗ ㉛

#115 ★   21/64

KANGASKHAN Level 40

HP 90 ◇

Retreat Cost ★ ★ ★

Weakness ✊   Resistance ◎

Fetch   ★

Draw a card.

Comet Punch   ★ ★ ★ ★   20x

Flip 4 coins. This attack does 20 damage times the number of heads.

Win from ③ ⑥ ⑦ ⑩ ⑭ ⑮ ㉖ ㉗ ㉛

#128 ♦ TAUROS Level 32 — 47/64

HP 60 ◇

Retreat Cost ✸ ✸

Weakness 👊 **Resistance** 👁

Stomp ✸ ✸ **20+**

Flip a coin. If heads, this attack does 20 damage plus 10 more damage; if tails, this attack does 20 damage.

Rampage ✸ ✸ ✸ **20+**

Does 20 damage plus 10 more damage for each damage counter on Tauros. Flip a coin. If tails, Tauros is now confused (after doing damage).

Win from ❶ ❽ ❾ ⓫ ⓭ ⓰ ⓲ ⑳ ㉙ ㉜

#132 ★ DITTO Level 19

HP 50 ◇

Retreat Cost ✸

Weakness 👊 **Resistance** 👁

Pound ✸ **10**

Morph ✸ ✸ ✸

Remove all damage counters from Ditto. For the rest of the game, replace Ditto with a copy of a Basic Pokémon card (other than Ditto) chosen at random from your deck. Ditto is no longer asleep, confused, paralyzed, poisoned, or anything else that might be the result of an attack (just as if you had evolved it).

GAME BOY ONLY

Win from ❹ ⓬ ⓱ ㉓ ㉔ ㉘

#133 ● EEVEE Level 12 — 51/64

HP 50 ◇

Evol. 1 Vaporeon
Evol. 1 Jolteon
Evol. 1 Flareon

Retreat Cost ✸

Weakness 👊 **Resistance** 👁

Tail Wag ✸

Flip a coin. If heads, the Defending Pokémon can't attack Eevee during your opponent's next turn. (Benching either Pokémon ends this effect.)

Quick Attack ✸ ✸ **10+**

Flip a coin. If heads, this attack does 10 damage plus 20 more damage; if tails, this attack does 10 damage.

Win from ❷ ❺ ⓳ ㉑ ㉒ ㉕ ㉚

#137 ♦ PORYGON Level 12 — 39/102

HP 30 ◇

Retreat Cost ✸

Weakness 👊 **Resistance** 👁

Conversion 1 ✸

If the Defending Pokémon has a Weakness, you may change it to a type of your choice other than Colorless.

Conversion 2 ✸ ✸

Change Porygon's Resistance to a type of your choice other than Colorless.

Win from ❹ ⓬ ⓱ ㉓ ㉔ ㉘

#143 ★ SNORLAX Level 20 — 27/64

HP 90 ◇

Retreat Cost ✸ ✸ ✸ ✸

Weakness 👊 **Resistance** 👁

Pokémon Power: Thick Skinned

Snorlax can't become asleep, confused, paralyzed, or poisoned. This power can't be used if Snorlax is already asleep, confused, or paralyzed.

Body Slam ✸ ✸ ✸ **30**

Flip a coin. If heads, the Defending Pokémon is now paralyzed.

Win from ❸ ❻ ❼ ❿ ⓮ ⓯ ㉖ ㉗ ㉛

#147 ♦ DRATINI Level 10 — 26/102

HP 40 ◇

Evol. 1 Dragonair
Evol. 2 Dragonite

Retreat Cost ✸

Weakness — **Resistance** 👁

Pound ✸ **10**

Win from ❶ ❽ ❾ ⓫ ⓭ ⓰ ⓲ ⑳ ㉙ ㉜

#148 ★   18/102

DRAGONAIR Level 33

HP 80   Basic **Dratini**
                Evol. 2 **Dragonite**

Retreat Cost ✴ ✴

Weakness—   **Resistance** 👁

Slam   ✴ ✴ ✴   **30x**

Flip 2 coins. This attack does 30 damage times the number of heads.

Hyper Beam   ✴ ✴ ✴ ✴   **20**

If the Defending Pokémon has any Energy Cards attached to it, choose 1 of them and discard it.

Win from ① ⑧ ⑨ ⑪ ⑬ ⑯ ⑱ ⑳ ㉙ ㉜

#149 ★   19/62

DRAGONITE Level 45

HP 100   Basic **Dratini**
                 Evol. 1 **Dragonair**

Retreat Cost ✴

Weakness —   **Resistance** ✊

Pokémon Power: Step In

Once during your turn (before your attack), if Dragonite is on your Bench, you may switch it with your Active Pokémon.

Slam   ✴ ✴ ✴ ✴   **40x**

Flip 2 coins. This attack does 40 damage times the number of heads.

Win from ① ⑧ ⑨ ⑪ ⑬ ⑯ ⑱ ⑳ ㉙ ㉜

TRAINER CARDS

◆   88/102

PROFESSOR OAK

Discard your hand, then draw 7 cards.

Win from ③ ⑥ ⑦ ⑩ ⑭ ⑮ ㉖ ㉗ ㉛

★   73/102

IMPOSTER PROFESSOR OAK

Your opponent shuffles his or her hand into his or her deck, then draws 7 cards.

Win from ④ ⑫ ⑰ ㉓ ㉔ ㉘

●   91/102

BILL

Draw 2 cards.

Win from ③ ⑥ ⑦ ⑩ ⑭ ⑮ ㉖ ㉗ ㉛

MR. FUJI

58/62

Choose a Pokémon on your Bench. Shuffle it and any cards attached to it into your deck.

Win from ① ⑧ ⑨ ⑪ ⑬ ⑯ ⑱ ⑳ ㉙ ㉜

LASS

75/102

You and your opponent show each other your hands, then shuffle all the Trainer Cards from your hands into your decks.

Win from ④ ⑫ ⑰ ㉓ ㉔ ㉘

POKéMON TRADER

77/102

Trade 1 of the Basic Pokémon or Evolution cards in your hand for 1 of the Basic Pokémon or Evolution cards from your deck. Show both cards to your opponent. Shuffle your deck afterward.

Win from ② ⑤ ⑲ ㉑ ㉒ ㉕ ㉚

POKéMON BREEDER

76/102

Put a Stage 2 Evolution card from your hand on the matching Basic Pokémon. You can only play this card when you would be allowed to evolve that Pokémon anyway.

Win from ② ⑤ ⑲ ㉑ ㉒ ㉕ ㉚

CLEFAIRY DOLL

70/102

Play Clefairy Doll as if it were a Basic Pokémon. While in play, Clefairy Doll counts as a Pokémon (instead of a Trainer card). Clefairy Doll has no attacks, can't retreat, and can't be asleep, confused, paralyzed, or poisoned. If Clefairy Doll is knocked out, it doesn't count as a knocked out Pokémon. At any time during your turn before your attack, you may discard Clefairy Doll.

HP 10

Win from ② ⑤ ⑲ ㉑ ㉒ ㉕ ㉚

MYSTERIOUS FOSSIL

62/62

Play Mysterious Fossil as if it were a Basic Pokémon. While in play, Mysterious Fossil counts as a Pokémon (instead of a Trainer Card). Mysterious Fossil has no attacks, can't retreat, and can't be asleep, confused, paralyzed, or poisoned. If Mysterious Fossil is knocked out, it doesn't count as a knocked out Pokémon. (Discard it anyway.) At any time during your turn before your attack, you may discard Mysterious Fossil from play.

HP 10

Win from ① ⑧ ⑨ ⑪ ⑬ ⑯ ⑱ ⑳ ㉙ ㉜

◆ 81/102

ENERGY RETRIEVAL

Trade 1 of the other cards in your hand for up to 2 basic Energy Cards from your discard pile.

Win from ② ⑤ ⑲ ㉑ ㉒ ㉕ ㉚

● 59/62

ENERGY SEARCH

Search your deck for a basic Energy Card and put it into your hand. Shuffle your deck afterward.

Win from ② ⑤ ⑲ ㉑ ㉒ ㉕ ㉚

● 92/102

ENERGY REMOVAL

Choose 1 Energy Card attached to 1 of your opponent's Pokémon and discard it.

Win from ① ⑧ ⑨ ⑪ ⑬ ⑯ ⑱ ⑳ ㉙ ㉜

★ 79/102

SUPER ENERGY REMOVAL

Discard 1 Energy Card attached to 1 of your own Pokémon in order to choose 1 of your opponent's Pokémon and up to 2 Energy Cards attached to it. Discard those Energy Cards.

Win from ④ ⑫ ⑰ ㉓ ㉔ ㉘

● 95/102

SWITCH

Switch 1 of your Benched Pokémon with your Active Pokémon.

Win from ③ ⑥ ⑦ ⑩ ⑭ ⑮ ㉖ ㉗ ㉛

◆ 85/102

POKéMON CENTER

Remove all damage counters from all of your own Pokémon with damage counters on them, then discard all Energy Cards attached to those Pokémon.

Win from ① ⑧ ⑨ ⑪ ⑬ ⑯ ⑱ ⑳ ㉙ ㉜

POKé BALL
64/64

Flip a coin. If heads, you may search your deck for any Basic Pokémon or Evolution card. Show that card to your opponent, then put it into your hand. Shuffle your deck afterward.

Win from ③ ⑥ ⑦ ⑩ ⑭ ⑮ ㉖ ㉗ ㉛

SCOOP UP
78/102

Choose 1 of your Pokémon in play and return its Basic Pokémon card to your hand. (Discard all cards attached to that card.)

Win from ③ ⑥ ⑦ ⑩ ⑭ ⑮ ㉖ ㉗ ㉛

COMPUTER SEARCH
71/102

Discard 2 of the other cards from your hand in order to search your deck for any card and put it into your hand. Shuffle your deck afterward.

Win from ③ ⑥ ⑦ ⑩ ⑭ ⑮ ㉖ ㉗ ㉛

POKéDEX
87/102

Look at up to 5 cards from the top of your deck and rearrange them as you like.

Win from ④ ⑫ ⑰ ㉓ ㉔ ㉘

PLUSPOWER
84/102

Attach PlusPower to your Active Pokémon. At the end of your turn, discard PlusPower. If this Pokémon's attack does damage to itself and the Defending Pokémon (after applying Weakness and Resistance), the attack does 10 more damage to both Pokémon.

Win from ③ ⑥ ⑦ ⑩ ⑭ ⑮ ㉖ ㉗ ㉛

DEFENDER
80/102

Attach Defender to 1 of your Pokémon. At the end of your opponent's next turn, discard Defender. Damage done to that Pokémon by attacks is reduced by 20 (after applying Weakness and Resistance).

Win from ③ ⑥ ⑦ ⑩ ⑭ ⑮ ㉖ ㉗ ㉛

ITEM FINDER

Discard 2 of the other cards from your hand in order to put a Trainer Card from your discard pile into your hand.

Win from ③ ⑥ ⑦ ⑩ ⑭ ⑮ ㉖ ㉗ ㉛

GUST OF WIND

Choose 1 of your opponent's Benched Pokémon and switch it with his or her Active Pokémon.

Win from ② ⑤ ⑲ ㉑ ㉒ ㉕ ㉚

DEVOLUTION SPRAY

Choose 1 of your own Pokémon in play and a Stage of Evolution. Discard all Evolution cards of that Stage or higher attached to that Pokémon. That Pokémon is no longer asleep, confused, paralyzed, poisoned, or anything else that might be the result of an attack (just as if you had evolved it).

Win from ④ ⑫ ⑰ ㉓ ㉔ ㉘

REVIVE

Put 1 Basic Pokémon card from your discard pile onto your Bench. Put damage counters on that Pokémon equal to half its HP (rounded down to the nearest 10). (You can't play Revive if your Bench is full.)

Win from ③ ⑥ ⑦ ⑩ ⑭ ⑮ ㉖ ㉗ ㉛

SUPER POTION

Discard 1 Energy Card attached to 1 of your own Pokémon in order to remove up to 4 damage counters from that Pokémon.

Win from ② ⑤ ⑲ ㉑ ㉒ ㉕ ㉚

POTION

Remove up to 2 damage counters from 1 of your Pokémon.

Win from ③ ⑥ ⑦ ⑩ ⑭ ⑮ ㉖ ㉗ ㉛

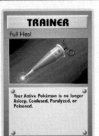

82/102

FULL HEAL

Your Active Pokémon is no longer asleep, confused, paralyzed, or poisoned.

Win from ③ ⑥ ⑦ ⑩ ⑭ ⑮ ㉖ ㉗ ㉛

83/102

MAINTENANCE

Shuffle 2 of the other cards from your hand into your deck in order to draw a card.

Win from ④ ⑫ ⑰ ㉓ ㉔ ㉘

86/102

POKÉMON FLUTE

Choose 1 Basic Pokémon card from your opponent's discard pile and put it onto his or her Bench. (You can't play Pokémon Flute if your opponent's Bench is full.)

Win from ② ⑤ ⑲ ㉑ ㉒ ㉕ ㉚

60/62

GAMBLER

Shuffle your hand into your deck. Flip a coin. If heads, draw 8 cards. If tails, draw 1 card.

Win from ④ ⑫ ⑰ ㉓ ㉔ ㉘

61/62

RECYCLE

Flip a coin. If heads, put a card in your discard pile on top of your deck.

Win from ④ ⑫ ⑰ ㉓ ㉔ ㉘

ENERGY CARDS

GRASS ENERGY
99/102

Grass-Type Pokémon require Grass Energy to use their attacks.

FIRE ENERGY
98/102

Power your Fire Pokémon's attacks with this type of Energy Card.

WATER ENERGY
102/102

If you are using a Water-Type Pokémon, be sure to use Water Energy.

LIGHTNING ENERGY
100/102

Lightning Energy Cards are used with Electric Pokémon.

PSYCHIC ENERGY
101/102

Attach this kind of energy to any Psychic Pokémon in your bench.

FIGHTING ENERGY
97/102

Your Fighting-Type Pokémon's attacks use Fighting Energy Cards.

DOUBLE COLORLESS ENERGY
96/102

This energy is attached to Colorless Pokémon, and can also be used to power other Pokémon's attacks if an energy type is not specified. Double Colorless Energy can also be attached to a Pokémon and then used as the energy to retreat, if the energy required to retreat is not specified.

PROMOTION CARDS

#59 ★

ARCANINE Level 34

HP 70 **Basic** Growlithe

Retreat Cost ✸
Weakness **Resistance** —

Quick Attack ✸ ✸ **10+**

Flip a coin. If heads, this attack does 10 damage plus 20 more damage; if tails, this attack does 10 damage.

Flames of Rage 🔥 🔥 **40+**

Discard 2 🔥 Energy Cards attached to Arcanine in order to use this attack. This attack does 40 damage plus 10 more damage for each damage counter on Arcanine.

GAME BOY ONLY

Exchange a level-31 Lapras for this card at the Water Club or win it at a Challenge Cup after you finish the regular game.

#25 ★ 63/102

PIKACHU Level 16

HP 60 **Evol. 1 Raichu**

Retreat Cost ✸
Weakness **Resistance** —

Growl ✸

If the Defending Pokémon attacks Pikachu during your opponent's next turn, any damage done by the attack is reduced by 10 (after applying Weakness and Resistance). (Benching or evolving either Pokémon ends this effect.)

Thundershock ⚡ ⚡ **20**

Flip a coin. If heads, the Defending Pokémon is now paralyzed.

Obtain this card at the Fighting Club in exchange for a level-26 Graveler.

#25 ★ 63/102

PIKACHU Level 13

HP 60 **Evol. 1 Raichu**

Retreat Cost ✸
Weakness **Resistance** —

Growl ✸

If the Defending Pokémon attacks Pikachu during your opponent's next turn, any damage done by the attack is reduced by 10 (after applying Weakness and Resistance). (Benching or evolving either Pokémon ends this effect.)

Thundershock ⚡ ⚡ **20**

Flip a coin. If heads, the Defending Pokémon is now paralyzed.

Win this card at a Challenge Cup tournament after you finish the regular game.

#25 ★ 42/102

SURFING PIKACHU Level 13

HP 50

Retreat Cost ✸
Weakness **Resistance** —

Surf 🌊 🌊 **30**

GAME BOY ONLY

Obtain this card from Ishihara in exchange for a level-34 Clefable.

#25 ★ 000/102

SURFING PIKACHU Level 13

HP 50

Retreat Cost ✸
Weakness **Resistance** —

Surf 🌊 🌊 **30**

GAME BOY ONLY

Obtain this card from Ishihara in exchange for a level-55 Chansey.

#25 ★

FLYING PIKACHU Level 12

HP 40

Retreat Cost

Weakness — **Resistance**

Thundershock **10**

Flip a coin. If heads, the Defending Pokémon is now paralyzed.

Fly **30**

Flip a coin. If heads, during your opponent's next turn, prevent all effects of attacks, including damage, done to Flying Pikachu. If tails, this attack does nothing (not even damage).

Obtain this card from Ishihara in exchange for a level-19 Ditto.

GAME BOY ONLY

#125 ★

ELECTABUZZ Level 20

HP 60

Retreat Cost

Weakness **Resistance** —

Light Screen

Whenever an attack does damage to Electabuzz (after applying Weakness and Resistance) during your opponent's next turn, that attack only does half the damage to Electabuzz (rounded down to the nearest 10). (Any other effects of attacks still happen.)

Quick Attack **10+**

Flip a coin. If heads, this attack does 10 damage plus 20 more damage; if tails, this attack does 10 damage.

Obtain this card at the Electric Club in exchange for a level-35 Electabuzz.

#79 ★

SLOWPOKE Level 9

HP 40 **Evol. 1 Slobro**

Retreat Cost

Weakness **Resistance** —

Headbutt **10**

Amnesia

Choose 1 of the Defending Pokémon's attacks. That Pokémon can't use that attack during your opponent's next turn.

Obtain this card at the Fire Club in exchange for Energy Cards.

GAME BOY ONLY

#150 ★

MEWTWO Level 60

HP 70

Retreat Cost

Weakness **Resistance** —

Energy Absorption

Energy Absorption Choose up to 2 Energy Cards from your discard pile and attach them to Mewtwo.

PsyBurn **40**

Win this card at a Challenge Cup tournament during or after the regular game.

#150 ★

MEWTWO Level 60

HP 70

Retreat Cost

Weakness **Resistance** —

Energy Absorption

Choose up to 2 Energy Cards from your discard pile and attach them to Mewtwo.

Psyburn **40**

Obtain this card from a person at the Psychic Club after you defeat the Club Master.

GAME BOY ONLY

#151 ★

MEW Level 8

HP 40

Retreat Cost

Weakness **Resistance** —

Pokémon Power: Neutralizing Shield

Prevent all effects of attacks, including damage, done to Mew by evolved Pokémon (including your own). This power stops working while Mew is asleep, confused, or paralyzed.

Psyshock **10**

Flip a coin. If heads, the Defending Pokémon is now paralyzed.

Win this card at a Challenge Cup tournament during or after the regular game.

GAME BOY ONLY

#39 ★

JIGGLYPUFF Level 12

HP 50   **Evol. 1 Wigglytuff**

Retreat Cost

Weakness   **Resistance**

First Aid

Remove 1 damage counter from Jigglypuff.

Double-edge   ★ ★ ★   **40**

Jigglypuff does 20 damage to itself.

Win this card at a Challenge Cup tournament after you finish the regular game.

TRAINER

IMAKUNI?

★

IMAKUNI?

Your Active Pokémon is now confused. Imakuni wants you to play him as a Basic Pokémon, but you can't. A mysterious creature not listed in the Pokédex. He asks kids around the world, "Who is cuter—Pikachu or me?"

GAME BOY ONLY

Win this card by defeating Imakuni twice.

TRAINER

SUPER ENERGY RETRIEVAL

★

SUPER ENERGY RETRIEVAL

Trade 2 of the other cards in your hand for up to basic 4 Energy Cards from your discard pile.

GAME BOY ONLY

Win this card by defeating Ronald a second time during the regular game.

LEGENDARY CARDS

POKéMON

MOLTRES

#146 ★

MOLTRES Level 37

HP 100

Retreat Cost ★ ★

Weakness —   **Resistance**

Pokémon Power: Firegiver

When you put Moltres into play during your turn (not during set-up), put from 1 to 4 (chosen at random) Energy Cards from your deck into your hand. Shuffle your deck afterward.

Dive Bomb   **70**

Flip a coin. If tails, this attack does nothing.

Defeat the Club Masters to win this card.

GAME BOY ONLY

POKéMON

ARTICUNO

#144 ★

ARTICUNO Level 37

HP 100

Retreat Cost ★ ★

Weakness —   **Resistance**

Pokémon Power: Quickfreeze

When you put Articuno into play during your turn (not during set-up), flip a coin. If heads, the Defending Pokémon is now paralyzed.

Ice Breath

Does 40 damage to 1 of your opponent's Pokémon chosen at random. Don't apply Weakness and Resistance for this attack. (Any other effects that would happen after applying Weakness and Resistance still happen.)

Defeat the Club Masters to win this card.

GAME BOY ONLY

POKéMON
ZAPDOS

#145

ZAPDOS Level 68

HP 100

Retreat Cost

Weakness — **Resistance**

Pokémon Power: Peal of Thunder

When you put Zapdos into play during your turn (not during set-up), do 30 damage to a Pokémon other than Zapdos chosen at random. (Don't apply Weakness and Resistance.)

BigThunder

Choose a Pokémon other than Zapdos at random. This attack does 70 damage to that Pokémon. Don't apply Weakness and Resistance for this attack. (Any other effects that would happen after applying Weakness and Resistance still happen.)

Defeat the Club Masters to win this card.

POKéMON
DRAGONITE

#149

DRAGONITE Level 41

HP 100 Basic **Dratini**
Evol. 1 **Dragonair**

Retreat Cost

Weakness — **Resistance**

Pokémon Power: Healing Wind

When you put Dragonite into play, remove 2 damage counters from each of your Pokémon. If a Pokémon has fewer damage counters than that, remove all of them from that Pokémon.

Slam   **30x**

Flip 2 coins. This attack does 30 damage times the number of heads.

Defeat the Club Masters to win this card.

ILLUSION CARDS

POKéMON
VENUSAUR

#3 ★

VENUSAUR Level 64

HP 100 Basic **Bulbasaur**
Evol. 1 **Ivysaur**

Retreat Cost

Weakness **Resistance** —

Pokémon Power: Solar Power

Once during your turn (before your attack), you may use this power. Your Active Pokémon and the Defending Pokémon are no longer asleep, confused, paralyzed, or poisoned. This power can't be used if Venusaur is asleep, confused, or paralyzed.

Mega Drain **40**

Remove a number of damage counters from Venusaur equal to half the damage done to the Defending Pokémon (after applying Weakness and Resistance) (rounded up to the nearest 10). If Venusaur has fewer damage counters than that, remove all of them.

Card Pop! will randomly produce this card.

POKéMON
MEW

#151 ★

MEW Level 15

HP 50

Retreat Cost —

Weakness **Resistance** —

Mystery Attack

Does a random amount of damage to the Defending Pokémon and may cause a random effect to the Defending Pokémon.

Card Pop! will randomly produce this card.

Quick Reference

Use this list as a quick way to check your card's level, type, weakness and resistance. For more detailed information about a specific card, check the page listed in the last column.

NAME	LEVEL	TYPE	WEAKNESS	RESISTANCE	PAGE #
Abra	10	Psychic	Psychic		64
Aerodactyl	28	Fighting	Grass	Fighting	71
Alakazam	42	Psychic	Psychic		64
Arbok	27	Grass	Psychic		48
Arcanine	34	Fire	Water		83
Arcanine	45	Fire	Water		55
Articuno	35	Water		Fighting	61
Articuno	37	Water		Fighting	85
Beedrill	32	Grass	Fire	Fighting	48
Bellsprout	11	Grass	Fire		51
Blastoise	52	Water	Lightning		56
Bulbasaur	13	Grass	Fire		47
Butterfree	28	Grass	Fire	Fighting	48
Caterpie	13	Grass	Fire		47
Chansey	55	Colorless	Fighting	Psychic	74
Charizard	76	Fire	Water	Fighting	54
Charmander	10	Fire	Water		53
Charmeleon	32	Fire	Water		54
Clefable	34	Colorless	Fighting	Psychic	72
Clefairy	14	Colorless	Fighting	Psychic	72
Cloyster	25	Water	Lightning		58
Cubone	13	Fighting	Grass	Lightning	69
Dewgong	42	Water	Lightning		58
Diglett	8	Fighting	Grass	Lightning	67
Ditto	19	Colorless	Fighting	Psychic	75
Dodrio	28	Colorless	Lightning	Fighting	74
Doduo	10	Colorless	Lightning	Fighting	74
Dragonair	33	Colorless		Psychic	76
Dragonite	41	Colorless		Fighting	86
Dragonite	45	Colorless		Fighting	76
Dratini	10	Colorless		Psychic	75

NAME	LEVEL	TYPE	WEAKNESS	RESISTANCE	PAGE #
Drowzee	12	Psychic	Psychic		66
Dugtrio	36	Fighting	Grass	Lightning	67
Eevee	12	Colorless	Fighting	Psychic	75
Ekans	10	Grass	Psychic		48
Electabuzz	20	Lightning	Fighting		84
Electabuzz	35	Lightning	Fighting		63
Electrode	35	Lightning	Fighting		63
Electrode	42	Lightning	Fighting		63
Exeggcute	14	Grass	Fire		52
Exeggutor	35	Grass	Fire		52
Farfetch'd	20	Colorless	Lightning	Fighting	74
Fearow	27	Colorless	Lightning	Fighting	72
Flareon	22	Fire	Water		55
Flareon	28	Fire	Water		56
Gastly	8	Psychic		Fighting	65
Gastly	17	Psychic		Fighting	65
Gengar	38	Psychic	Psychic	Fighting	66
Geodude	16	Fighting	Grass		68
Gloom	22	Grass	Fire		50
Golbat	29	Grass	Psychic	Fighting	50
Goldeen	12	Water	Lightning		59
Golduck	27	Water	Lightning		57
Golem	36	Fighting	Grass		69
Graveler	29	Fighting	Grass		69
Grimer	17	Grass	Psychic		52
Growlithe	18	Fire	Water		54
Gyarados	41	Water	Grass	Fighting	60
Haunter	17	Psychic		Fighting	65
Haunter	22	Psychic		Fighting	65
Hitmonchan	33	Fighting	Psychic		70
Hitmonlee	30	Fighting	Psychic		70
Horsea	19	Water	Lightning		59
Hypno	36	Psychic	Psychic		66
Ivysaur	20	Grass	Fire		47
Jigglypuff	12	Colorless	Fighting	Psychic	85
Jigglypuff	13	Colorless	Fighting	Psychic	73
Jigglypuff	14	Colorless	Fighting	Psychic	73
Jolteon	24	Lightning	Fighting		63
Jolteon	29	Lightning	Fighting		63

NAME	LEVEL	TYPE	WEAKNESS	RESISTANCE	PAGE #
Jynx	23	Psychic	Psychic		66
Kabuto	9	Fighting	Grass		70
Kabutops	30	Fighting	Grass		70
Kadabra	38	Psychic	Psychic		64
Kakuna	23	Grass	Fire		48
Kangaskhan	40	Colorless	Fighting	Psychic	74
Kingler	27	Water	Lightning		59
Koffing	13	Grass	Psychic		52
Krabby	20	Water	Lightning		58
Lapras	31	Water	Lightning		60
Lickitung	26	Colorless	Fighting	Psychic	74
Machamp	67	Fighting	Psychic		68
Machoke	40	Fighting	Psychic		68
Machop	20	Fighting	Psychic		68
Magikarp	8	Water	Lightning		60
Magmar	24	Fire	Water		55
Magmar	31	Fire	Water		55
Magnemite	13	Lightning	Fighting		62
Magnemite	15	Lightning	Fighting		62
Magneton	28	Lightning	Fighting		62
Magneton	35	Lightning	Fighting		62
Mankey	7	Fighting	Psychic		68
Marowak	26	Fighting	Grass	Lightning	69
Marowak	32	Fighting	Grass	Lightning	69
Meowth	14	Colorless	Fighting	Psychic	73
Meowth	15	Colorless	Fighting	Psychic	73
Metapod	21	Grass	Fire		47
Mew	8	Psychic	Psychic		84
Mew	15	Psychic	Psychic		86
Mew	23	Psychic	Psychic		67
Mewtwo	53	Psychic	Psychic		66
Mewtwo	60	Psychic	Psychic		84
Mewtwo	60	Psychic	Psychic		84
Moltres	35	Fire		Fighting	56
Moltres	37	Fire		Fighting	85
Mr. Mime	28	Psychic	Psychic		66
Muk	34	Grass	Psychic		52
Nidoking	48	Grass	Psychic		49
Nidoqueen	43	Grass	Psychic		49

NAME	LEVEL	TYPE	WEAKNESS	RESISTANCE	PAGE #
Nidoran ♀	13	Grass	Psychic		49
Nidoran ♂	20	Grass	Psychic		49
Nidorina	24	Grass	Psychic		49
Nidorino	25	Grass	Psychic		49
Ninetales	32	Fire	Water		54
Ninetales	35	Fire	Water		54
Oddish	8	Grass	Fire		50
Omanyte	19	Water	Grass		61
Omastar	32	Water	Grass		61
Onix	12	Fighting	Grass		69
Paras	8	Grass	Fire		50
Parasect	28	Grass	Fire		51
Persian	25	Colorless	Fighting	Psychic	73
Pidgeot	38	Colorless	Lightning	Fighting	71
Pidgeot	40	Colorless	Lightning	Fighting	71
Pidgeotto	36	Colorless	Lightning	Fighting	71
Pidgey	8	Colorless	Lightning	Fighting	71
Pikachu	12	Lightning	Fighting		61
Pikachu (Fly)	12	Lightning		Fighting	84
Pikachu (Surf)	13	Lightning	Fighting		83
Pikachu (Surf)	13	Lightning	Fighting		83
Pikachu	14	Lightning	Fighting		61
Pikachu	16	Lightning	Fighting		83
Pikachu	16	Lightning	Fighting		83
Pinsir	24	Grass	Fire		53
Poliwag	13	Water	Grass		57
Poliwhirl	28	Water	Grass		57
Poliwrath	48	Water	Grass		57
Ponyta	10	Fire	Water		55
Porygon	12	Colorless	Fighting	Psychic	75
Primeape	35	Fighting	Psychic		68
Psyduck	15	Water	Lightning		57
Raichu	40	Lightning	Fighting		62
Raichu	45	Lightning	Fighting		62
Rapidash	33	Fire	Water		55
Raticate	41	Colorless	Fighting	Psychic	72
Rattata	9	Colorless	Fighting	Psychic	72
Rhydon	48	Fighting	Grass	Lightning	70
Rhyhorn	18	Fighting	Grass	Lightning	70

NAME	LEVEL	TYPE	WEAKNESS	RESISTANCE	PAGE #
Sandshrew	12	Fighting	Grass	Lightning	67
Sandslash	33	Fighting	Grass	Lightning	67
Scyther	25	Grass	Fire	Fighting	53
Seadra	23	Water	Lightning		59
Seaking	28	Water	Lightning		59
Seel	12	Water	Lightning		58
Shellder	8	Water	Lightning		58
Slowbro	26	Psychic	Psychic		65
Slowpoke	9	Psychic	Psychic		84
Slowpoke	18	Psychic	Psychic		65
Snorlax	20	Colorless	Fighting	Psychic	75
Spearow	13	Colorless	Lightning	Fighting	72
Squirtle	8	Water	Lightning		56
Starmie	28	Water	Lightning		60
Staryu	15	Water	Lightning		59
Tangela	8	Grass	Fire		53
Tangela	12	Grass	Fire		53
Tauros	32	Colorless	Fighting	Psychic	75
Tentacool	10	Water	Lightning		57
Tentacruel	21	Water	Lightning		58
Vaporeon	29	Water	Lightning		60
Vaporeon	42	Water	Lightning		60
Venomoth	28	Grass	Fire	Fighting	51
Venonat	12	Grass	Fire		51
Venusaur	64	Grass	Fire		86
Venusaur	67	Grass	Fire		47
Victreebel	42	Grass	Fire		51
Vileplume	35	Grass	Fire		50
Voltorb	10	Lightning	Fighting		63
Vulpix	11	Fire	Water		54
Wartortle	22	Water	Lightning		56
Weedle	12	Grass	Fire		48
Weepinbell	28	Grass	Fire		51
Weezing	27	Grass	Psychic		52
Wigglytuff	36	Colorless	Fighting	Psychic	73
Zapdos	40	Lightning		Fighting	64
Zapdos	64	Lightning		Fighting	64
Zapdos	68	Lightning		Fighting	86
Zubat	10	Grass	Psychic	Fighting	50

TRAINER CARDS	PAGE #
Bill	76
Clefairy Doll	77
Defender	79
Devolution Spray	80
Energy Removal	78
Energy Retrieval	78
Energy Search	78
Full Heal	81
Gambler	81
Gust of Wind	80
Imakuni ?	85
Imposter Professor Oak	76
Item Finder	80
Lass	77
Maintenance	81
Mr. Fuji	77
Mysterious Fossil	77

TRAINER CARDS	PAGE #
PC Net	79
PlusPower	79
Poké Ball	79
Pokédex	79
Poké Flute	81
Pokémon Breeder	77
Pokémon Center	78
Pokémon Trader	77
Potion	80
Professor Oak	76
Recycle	81
Revive	80
Scoop Up	79
Super Energy Removal	78
Super Energy Retrieval	85
Super Potion	80
Switch	78

BOOSTER PACK LIST

#1 COLOSSEUM

Win from ③ ⑥ ⑦ ⑩ ⑭ ⑮ ㉖ ㉗ ㉛

Pokémon Cards

NAME	Level	Rarity	NAME	Level	Rarity	NAME	Level	Rarity
GRASS			Goldeen	12	●	Hitmonchan	33	★
Nidoran ♂	20	●	Seaking	28	♦	**PSYCHIC**		
Nidorino	25	♦	Staryu	15	●	Abra	10	●
Tangela	12	●	Magikarp	8	♦	Kadabra	38	♦
Scyther	25	★	Gyarados	41	★	**COLORLESS**		
Pinsir	24	★	**LIGHTNING**			Rattata	9	●
FIRE			Pikachu	12	●	Raticate	41	♦
Charmander	10	●	Raichu	40	★	Jigglypuff	14	●
Charmeleon	32	♦	Magnemite	13	●	Wigglytuff	36	★
Growlithe	18	♦	Magneton	28	★	Meowth	14	●
Arcanine	45	♦	Electabuzz	35	★	Chansey	55	★
Ponyta	10	●	Zapdos	64	★	Kangaskhan	40	★
Magmar	24	♦	**FIGHTING**			Snorlax	20	★
WATER			Diglett	8	●			
Seel	12	♦	Dugtrio	36	★			
Dewgong	42	♦	Machop	20	●			

Trainer Cards

NAME	Rarity
Professor Oak	♦
Bill	●
Switch	●
Poké Ball	●
Scoop Up	★
Computer Search	★
PlusPower	♦
Defender	♦
Item Finder	★
Potion	●
Full Heal	♦
Revive	♦

#2 EVOLUTION

Win from ② ⑤ ⑲ ㉑ ㉒ ㉕ ㉚

Pokémon Cards

NAME	Level	Rarity	NAME	Level	Rarity	NAME	Level	Rarity
GRASS			Rapidash	33	♦	Machamp	67	★
Bulbasaur	13	●	Flareon	28	★	Geodude	16	●
Ivysaur	20	♦	**WATER**			Graveler	29	♦
Venusaur	67	★	Squirtle	8	●	Golem	36	♦
Caterpie	13	●	Wartortle	22	♦	Cubone	13	●
Metapod	21	●	Blastoise	52	★	Marowak	32	♦
Butterfree	28	♦	Krabby	20	●	**PSYCHIC**		
Weedle	12	●	Kingler	27	♦	Gastly	8	●
Kakuna	23	♦	Starmie	28	●	Haunter	22	♦
Beedrill	32	★	Vaporeon	42	★	Gengar	38	★
Nidoking	48	★	**LIGHTNING**			Jynx	23	♦
Bellsprout	11	●	Jolteon	29	★	**COLORLESS**		
Weepinbell	28	♦	**FIGHTING**			Pidgey	8	●
Victreebel	42	★	Sandshrew	12	●	Pidgeotto	36	★
FIRE			Sandslash	33	♦	Pidgeot	40	★
Charizard	76	★	Machoke	40	♦	Jigglypuff	13	●

NAME	Level	Rarity
Eevee	12	●

Trainer Cards

NAME	Level	Rarity
Pokémon Trader		★
Pokémon Breeder		★
Clefairy Doll		★
Energy Retrieval		♦
Energy Search		●
Gust of Wind		●
Super Potion		♦
Pokémon Flute		♦

#3 MYSTERY

Win from ① ⑧ ⑨ ⑪ ⑬ ⑯ ⑱ ⑳ ㉙ ㉜

Pokémon Cards

NAME	Level	Rarity	NAME	Level	Rarity	NAME	Level	Rarity
GRASS			Cloyster	25	♦	Kabuto	9	●
Nidoran ♀	13	●	Lapras	31	★	Kabutops	30	★
Nidorina	24	♦	Vaporeon	29	♦	Aerodactyl	28	★
Nidoqueen	43	★	Omanyte	19	●	**PSYCHIC**		
Oddish	8	●	Omastar	32	♦	Alakazam	42	★
Gloom	22	♦	Articuno	35	★	Drowzee	12	●
Vileplume	35	★	**LIGHTNING**			Mew	23	★
Paras	8	●	Pikachu	14	●	**COLORLESS**		
Parasect	28	♦	Raichu	45	★	Clefairy	14	★
Exeggcute	14	●	Voltorb	10	●	Meowth	15	●
Exeggutor	35	♦	Electrode	42	★	Persian	25	♦
FIRE			Jolteon	24	♦	Farfetch'd	20	♦
Vulpix	11	●	Zapdos	40	★	Lickitung	26	♦
Ninetales	32	★	**FIGHTING**			Tauros	32	♦
Flareon	22	♦	Mankey	7	●	Dratini	10	♦
Moltres	35	★	Primeape	35	♦	Dragonair	33	★
WATER			Rhyhorn	18	●	Dragonite	45	★
Shellder	8	●	Rhydon	48	♦			

Trainer Cards

NAME	Rarity
Mr. Fuji	♦
Mysterious Fossil	●
Energy Removal	●
Pokémon Center	♦

Energy Card

NAME	Rarity
Double Colorless Energy	♦

#4 LABORATORY

Win from ④ ⑫ ⑰ ㉓ ㉔ ㉘

Pokémon Cards

NAME	Level	Rarity	NAME	Level	Rarity	NAME	Level	Rarity
GRASS			Golduck	27	♦	**PSYCHIC**		
Ekans	10	●	Poliwag	13	●	Slowpoke	18	●
Arbok	27	♦	Poliwhirl	28	♦	Slowbro	26	♦
Zubat	10	●	Poliwrath	48	★	Gastly	17	♦
Golbat	29	♦	Tentacool	10	●	Haunter	17	★
Venonat	12	●	Tentacruel	21	♦	Hypno	36	★
Venomoth	28	★	Horsea	19	●	Mr. Mime	28	★
Grimer	17	●	Seadra	23	♦	Mewtwo	53	★
Muk	34	★	**LIGHTNING**			**COLORLESS**		
Koffing	13	●	Magnemite	15	●	Pidgeot	38	★
Weezing	27	♦	Magneton	35	★	Spearow	13	●
Tangela	8	●	Electrode	35	★	Fearow	27	♦
FIRE			**FIGHTING**			Clefable	34	★
Ninetales	35	★	Onix	12	●	Doduo	10	●
Magmar	31	♦	Marowak	26	♦	Dodrio	28	♦
WATER			Hitmonlee	30	★	Ditto	19	★
Psyduck	15	●				Porygon	12	♦

Trainer Cards

NAME	Rarity
Imposter Professor Oak	★
Lass	★
Super Energy Removal	★
Pokédex	♦
Devolution Spray	★
Maintenance	♦
Gambler	●
Recycle	●

First
Autodeck Machine

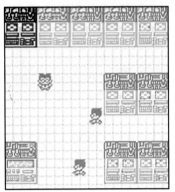

In this next section, we'll take a look at all the decks that you can create with Dr. Mason's amazing Autodeck Machines. We'll examine each deck, discuss potential strategies you can use with it and give you tips on tweaking it to suit different combat situations. We'll start with the first Autodeck Machine, which requires no medal to operate. Keep in mind that the "friends" decks shown here are different from the ones Dr. Mason offers you at the beginning of the game.

Charmander & Friends Deck

This deck suffers from the same malady as most of these early machine-made decks: too many different kinds of energy/Pokémon. Focus on just one or two types, maybe the Fire-types backed up by the Colorless-types.

TYPE	NAME	LEVEL	# OF CARDS	WEAKNESS
🍃	Caterpie	13	2	🔥
🍃	➤Metapod	21	1	🔥
🔥	Charmander	10	2	💧
🔥	➤Charmeleon	32	1	💧
🔥	➤Charizard	76	1	💧
🔥	Growlithe	18	2	💧
🔥	➤Arcanine	45	1	💧
💧	Seel	12	2	⚡
💧	➤Dewgong	42	1	⚡
💧	Goldeen	12	2	⚡
💧	➤Seaking	28	1	⚡
★	Rattata	9	2	👊
★	➤Raticate	41	1	👊
🔥	Ponyta	10	2	💧
🔥	Magmar	24	1	💧
🍃	Nidoran♀	13	2	👁
🍃	Nidoran♂	20	1	👁
🍃	Pinsir	24	1	🔥
★	Meowth	14	1	👊

ENERGY CARDS	# OF CARDS
Grass Energy	8
Fire Energy	10
Water Energy	6

TRAINER CARDS	# OF CARDS
Professor Oak	1
Bill	2
Switch	1
Computer Search	1
PlusPower	1
Potion	2
Full Heal	1

Squirtle & Friends Deck

This deck can be a good base for a Water-type-only deck. Use Blastoise's Rain Dance Pokémon Power to attach extra Energy Cards to Dewgong. You may be able to unleash a 50-point Aurora Beam attack a turn or two early.

TYPE	NAME	LEVEL	# OF CARDS	WEAKNESS
🔥	Charmander	10	2	💧
🔥	➤Charmeleon	32	1	💧
🔥	Growlithe	18	1	💧
🔥	➤Arcanine	45	1	💧
💧	Squirtle	8	2	⚡
💧	➤Wartortle	22	1	⚡
💧	➤Blastoise	52	1	⚡
💧	Seel	12	2	⚡
💧	➤Dewgong	42	1	⚡
💧	Goldeen	12	1	⚡
💧	➤Seaking	28	1	⚡
💧	Staryu	15	1	⚡
💧	➤Starmie	28	1	⚡
⚡	Magnemite	13	1	👊
⚡	➤Magneton	28	1	👊
★	Rattata	9	2	👊
★	➤Raticate	41	1	👊
💧	Lapras	31	1	⚡
⚡	Pikachu	12	2	👊
🔥	Magmar	24	1	💧
⚡	Electabuzz	35	1	👊
★	Meowth	14	1	👊

ENERGY CARDS	# OF CARDS
Fire Energy	8
Water Energy	11
Lightning Energy	6

TRAINER CARDS	# OF CARDS
Professor Oak	1
Bill	1
Switch	1
Poké Ball	1
Scoop Up	1
Item Finder	1
Potion	1
Full Heal	1

Bulbasaur & Friends Deck

The obvious strategy is to focus on the Grass-types, especially the Nidoran♀ and Bulbasaur lines. Use Nidoran♀'s Call for Family to fill the bench quickly and Venusaur's Energy Trans to shift Energy Cards as needed.

TYPE	NAME	LEVEL	# OF CARDS	WEAKNESS
🍃	Bulbasaur	13	2	🔥
🍃	➤Ivysaur	20	1	🔥
🍃	➤Venusaur	67	1	🔥
🍃	Nidoran♂	20	2	👁
🍃	➤Nidorino	25	1	👁
⚡	Pikachu	12	2	👊
⚡	➤Raichu	40	1	👊
👁	Abra	10	2	👁
👁	➤Kadabra	38	1	👁
👁	Gastly	8	2	—
👁	➤Haunter	22	1	—
⚡	Magnemite	13	1	👊
⚡	Electabuzz	35	1	👊
🍃	Nidoran♀	13	2	👁
🍃	Tangela	12	1	🔥
👁	Jynx	23	1	👁
✦	Jigglypuff	14	1	👊
✦	Meowth	14	1	👊
✦	Kangaskhan	40	1	👊

ENERGY CARDS	# OF CARDS
Grass Energy	9
Lightning Energy	8
Psychic Energy	6

TRAINER CARDS	# OF CARDS
Professor Oak	1
Bill	1
Switch	1
Poké Ball	1
PlusPower	2
Defender	1
Gust of Wind	1
Potion	2
Full Heal	2

Psychic Machamp Deck

A Psychic-type/Fighting-type collaboration is an interesting idea. Unless your opponent has a deck heavy on Psychic-types, you should do fine. Focus on the first four Pokémon groups on the list and beef up your Trainer Card list a bit.

TYPE	NAME	LEVEL	# OF CARDS	WEAKNESS
👊	Diglett	8	2	🍃
👊	➤Dugtrio	36	1	🍃
👊	Machop	20	2	👁
👊	➤Machoke	40	1	👁
👊	➤Machamp	67	1	👁
👁	Abra	10	2	👁
👁	➤Kadabra	38	1	👁
👁	➤Alakazam	42	1	👁
👁	Gastly	8	2	—
👁	➤Haunter	22	1	—
👁	➤Gengar	38	1	—
✦	Pidgey	8	2	⚡
✦	➤Pidgeotto	36	1	⚡
✦	➤Pidgeot	40	1	⚡
✦	Rattata	9	2	👊
✦	➤Raticate	41	1	👊
👊	Onix	12	1	🍃
👊	Hitmonlee	30	1	👁
👊	Hitmonchan	33	1	👁
👁	Mr. Mime	28	1	👁
👁	Jynx	23	1	👁
👁	Mew	23	1	👁

ENERGY CARDS	# OF CARDS
Fighting Energy	12
Psychic Energy	12

TRAINER CARDS	# OF CARDS
Professor Oak	1
Bill	2
Switch	1
Gust of Wind	1
Potion	2
Full Heal	1

Water-Beetle Deck

See how a Beedrill-Poliwrath combo performs against a Fighting-type deck. Beedrill's poisonous attacks would complement Poliwrath's pummeling power. Use Victreebel to force opponents to stay in the arena or retreat.

TYPE	NAME	LEVEL	# OF CARDS	WEAKNESS
🍃	Weedle	12	2	🔥
🍃	➤Kakuna	23	1	🔥
🍃	➤Beedrill	32	1	🔥
🍃	Nidoran♂	20	2	👁
🍃	➤Nidorino	25	1	👁
🍃	➤Nidoking	48	1	👁
🍃	Bellsprout	11	2	🔥
🍃	➤Weepinbell	28	1	🔥
🍃	➤Victreebel	42	1	🔥
💧	Poliwag	13	2	🍃
💧	➤Poliwhirl	28	1	🍃
💧	➤Poliwrath	48	1	🍃
💧	Krabby	20	2	⚡
💧	➤Kingler	27	1	⚡
💧	Magikarp	8	2	⚡
💧	➤Gyarados	41	1	⚡
🍃	Scyther	25	1	🔥
💧	Lapras	31	1	⚡
💧	Articuno	35	1	—
✦	Lickitung	26	1	👊
✦	Kangaskhan	40	1	👊
✦	Tauros	32	1	👊

ENERGY CARDS	# OF CARDS
Grass Energy	14
Water Energy	10

TRAINER CARDS	# OF CARDS
Professor Oak	1
Bill	2
Energy Retrieval	1
Energy Search	1
Switch	1
PlusPower	1
Full Heal	1

Grass Medal
Autodeck Machine

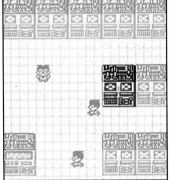

Medal: Grass Medal
From: Nikki ❹

As you'd expect, the Grass Medal activates this Autodeck Machine. These decks show better focus in Trainer Cards, though there are a few stray singles still lingering here and there (we recommend using two or more of any card). The Pokémon selection could also use some tightening up, but at least you have many options to choose from.

Insect Collection Deck

The focus is on Grass- and Bug-types, so expect a lot of paralyzing, confusing and sleep-inducing attacks. If you want to trim the fat, the Paras line should be the first to go. Don't underestimate Venomoth: confusion and poison together!

TYPE	NAME	LEVEL	# OF CARDS	WEAKNESS
🍃	Caterpie	13	3	🔥
🍃	▶Metapod	21	2	🔥
🍃	▶Butterfree	28	1	🔥
🍃	Weedle	12	3	🔥
🍃	▶Kakuna	23	2	🔥
🍃	▶Beedrill	32	1	🔥
🍃	Paras	8	4	🔥
🍃	▶Parasect	28	3	🔥
🍃	Venonat	12	2	🔥
🍃	▶Venomoth	28	1	🔥
🍃	Scyther	25	1	🔥
🍃	Pinsir	24	1	🔥

ENERGY CARDS	# OF CARDS
Grass Energy	24
TRAINER CARDS	**# OF CARDS**
Bill	2
Pokémon Breeder	2
Switch	2
Poké Ball	2
Pokédex	2
Potion	2

Jungle Deck

Lots of power, but not a whole lot of focus. Pick your favorite side effect and focus on that, for example, switching Pokémon from arena to Bench (Victreebel and Arbok), recovering damage (Golbat and Vileplume), and so on.

TYPE	NAME	LEVEL	# OF CARDS	WEAKNESS
🍃	Ekans	10	2	👁
🍃	▶Arbok	27	1	👁
🍃	Zubat	10	2	👁
🍃	▶Golbat	29	1	👁
🍃	Oddish	8	2	🔥
🍃	▶Gloom	22	1	🔥
🍃	▶Vileplume	35	1	🔥
🍃	Paras	8	2	🔥
🍃	▶Parasect	28	1	🔥
🍃	Venonat	12	2	🔥
🍃	▶Venomoth	28	1	🔥
🍃	Bellsprout	11	2	🔥
🍃	▶Weepinbell	28	1	🔥
🍃	▶Victreebel	42	1	🔥
🍃	Pinsir	24	1	🔥
✴	Lickitung	26	1	👊
✴	Kangaskhan	40	1	👊

ENERGY CARDS	# OF CARDS
Grass Energy	25
Double Colorless Energy	1
TRAINER CARDS	**# OF CARDS**
Bill	2
Poké Ball	1
PlusPower	2
Defender	2
Potion	2
Full Heal	1
Switch	1

Flower Garden Deck

Take a cue from Tangela and try this two-pronged attack: First poison your opponent and then try to paralyze it every turn after that. Several Energy Removal Cards will help ensure that your foes won't escape to the bench.

TYPE	NAME	LEVEL	# OF CARDS	WEAKNESS
🍃	Bulbasaur	13	3	🔥
🍃	▶Ivysaur	20	2	🔥
🍃	▶Venusaur	67	2	🔥
🍃	Oddish	8	3	🔥
🍃	▶Gloom	22	2	🔥
🍃	▶Vileplume	35	2	🔥
🍃	Bellsprout	11	2	🔥
🍃	▶Weepinbell	28	1	🔥
🍃	▶Victreebel	42	1	🔥
🍃	Tangela	8	2	🔥
🍃	Tangela	12	1	🔥
★	Lickitung	26	2	👊

ENERGY CARDS	# OF CARDS
Grass Energy	24
Double Colorless Energy	2

TRAINER CARDS	# OF CARDS
Pokémon Trader	2
Pokémon Breeder	3
Energy Search	1
Switch	2
Potion	2
Full Heal	1

Kaleidoscope Deck

With the ability to change Venomoth's type, your opponent's weakness, not to mention Ditto's entire profile, this deck will be able to meet most any threat. The only worry is a possible energy shortage, but Energy Search should help.

TYPE	NAME	LEVEL	# OF CARDS	WEAKNESS
🍃	Venonat	12	3	🔥
🍃	▶Venomoth	28	2	🔥
★	Eevee	12	4	👊
🔥	▶Flareon	22	1	💧
🔥	▶Flareon	28	1	💧
💧	▶Vaporeon	29	1	⚡
💧	▶Vaporeon	42	1	⚡
⚡	▶Jolteon	24	1	👊
⚡	▶Jolteon	29	1	👊
★	Ditto	19	4	👊
★	Porygon	12	4	👊

ENERGY CARDS	# OF CARDS
Grass Energy	10
Fire Energy	4
Water Energy	4
Lightning Energy	4
Double Colorless Energy	3

TRAINER CARDS	# OF CARDS
Bill	2
Mr. Fuji	2
Energy Search	2
Switch	4
Gust of Wind	2

Flower Power Deck

Remember the Energy Overload combo we discussed earlier in this guide? Use Venusaur's Energy Trans power to shift Energy Cards to Exeggutor, and then set off Exeggutor's Big Eggsplosion attack. Light the fuse, baby!

TYPE	NAME	LEVEL	# OF CARDS	WEAKNESS
🍃	Bulbasaur	13	4	🔥
🍃	▶Ivysaur	20	3	🔥
🍃	▶Venusaur	67	2	🔥
🍃	Oddish	8	4	🔥
🍃	▶Gloom	22	3	🔥
🍃	▶Vileplume	35	2	🔥
🍃	Exeggcute	14	4	🔥
🍃	▶Exeggutor	35	3	🔥

ENERGY CARDS	# OF CARDS
Grass Energy	18
Psychic Energy	4

TRAINER CARDS	# OF CARDS
Professor Oak	2
Bill	3
Pokémon Breeder	2
Energy Retrieval	2
Switch	2
Potion	2

Fire Medal
Autodeck Machine

Medal: Fire Medal
From: Ken 8

Now this is more like it! The decks are slowly becoming leaner and more focused, and more complex strategies are beginning to show in the combinations of cards. Of course, you should still feel free to tweak your decks as much as you like and experiment with different tactics. There are hundreds, perhaps thousands of combat possibilities!

Replace 'Em All Deck

Try this card combo: Use level-40 Pidgeot's Hurricane to force the defender and its attached cards back into your opponent's hand. On your next turn, use Lass or Imposter Prof. Oak to make your opponent return cards to his or her deck.

TYPE	NAME	LEVEL	# OF CARDS	WEAKNESS
🔥	Vulpix	11	4	💧
🔥	▶Ninetales	32	2	💧
🔥	▶Ninetales	35	1	💧
🔥	Growlithe	18	4	💧
🔥	▶Arcanine	34	1	💧
🔥	▶Arcanine	45	1	💧
★	Pidgey	8	4	⚡
★	▶Pidgeotto	36	3	⚡
★	▶Pidgeot	38	1	⚡
★	▶Pidgeot	40	1	⚡
★	Doduo	10	3	⚡
★	▶Dodrio	28	2	⚡

ENERGY CARDS	# OF CARDS
Fire Energy	24

TRAINER CARDS	# OF CARDS
Professor Oak	2
Imposter Professor Oak	2
Lass	2
Gust of Wind	3

Chari-saur Deck

This deck takes advantage of the Energy Crisis Card combo we showed you back on page 17. It also includes Eevee and Flareon for combat support. You might trade in one of the Pokémon Trader Cards for another Energy Removal.

TYPE	NAME	LEVEL	# OF CARDS	WEAKNESS
🌿	Bulbasaur	13	4	🔥
🌿	▶Ivysaur	20	3	🔥
🌿	▶Venusaur	67	2	🔥
🔥	Charmander	10	4	💧
🔥	▶Charmeleon	32	3	💧
🔥	▶Charizard	76	2	💧
★	Eevee	12	4	👊
🔥	▶Flareon	22	3	💧

ENERGY CARDS	# OF CARDS
Grass Energy	12
Fire Energy	10

TRAINER CARDS	# OF CARDS
Bill	2
Pokémon Trader	3
Pokémon Breeder	3
Energy Retrieval	2
Energy Removal	1
Potion	2

Traffic Light Deck

This is mainly a straightforward, damage-dealing deck that could use a bit of tweaking. If you cut Vaporeon and Pikachu and exchange the Water Energy for Fire Energy, Electric Energy and a few Trainer Cards, you'll be in business.

TYPE	NAME	LEVEL	# OF CARDS	WEAKNESS
🔥	Charmander	10	3	🔵
🔥	➤Charmeleon	32	2	🔵
🔥	Ponyta	10	3	🔵
🔥	➤Rapidash	33	2	🔵
★	Eevee	12	4	👊
🔥	➤Flareon	22	2	🔵
💧	➤Vaporeon	29	2	⚡
⚡	➤Jolteon	24	2	👊
⚡	Voltorb	10	3	👊
⚡	➤Electrode	42	2	👊
⚡	Pikachu	12	2	👊

ENERGY CARDS	# OF CARDS
Fire Energy	10
Water Energy	8
Lightning Energy	8

TRAINER CARDS	# OF CARDS
Energy Search	2
Switch	2
PlusPower	3

Fire Pokémon Deck

Again, this is just a straightforward damage-dealer that takes advantage of the range of Fire-based attacks. Exchange the single Trainer Cards for doubles of ones you like best (a little Potion and Full Heal never hurt, you know).

TYPE	NAME	LEVEL	# OF CARDS	WEAKNESS
🔥	Charmander	10	3	🔵
🔥	➤Charmeleon	32	2	🔵
🔥	➤Charizard	76	1	🔵
🔥	Vulpix	11	3	🔵
🔥	➤Ninetales	32	1	🔵
🔥	➤Ninetales	35	1	🔵
🔥	Growlithe	18	2	🔵
🔥	➤Arcanine	45	1	🔵
🔥	Ponyta	10	2	🔵
🔥	➤Rapidash	33	1	🔵
★	Eevee	12	3	👊
🔥	➤Flareon	22	1	🔵
🔥	➤Flareon	28	1	🔵
🔥	Magmar	24	1	🔵
🔥	Magmar	31	1	🔵
🔥	Moltres	35	1	—

ENERGY CARDS	# OF CARDS
Fire Energy	24
Double Colorless Energy	2

TRAINER CARDS	# OF CARDS
Professor Oak	1
Bill	2
Pokémon Trader	1
Pokémon Breeder	1
Energy Retrieval	1
Super Energy Retrieval	1
Switch	1
Gust of Wind	1

Fire Charge Deck

These Pokémon dish it out, but they can take it, too. Though your creatures will hurt themselves as well as their opponents, your Energy Retrieval Cards and Recycle Cards will help ensure that your team will return to fight again.

TYPE	NAME	LEVEL	# OF CARDS	WEAKNESS
🔥	Growlithe	18	4	🔵
🔥	➤Arcanine	45	3	🔵
★	Jigglypuff	12	3	👊
★	Jigglypuff	14	1	👊
★	➤Wigglytuff	36	1	👊
🔥	Magmar	24	2	🔵
★	Chansey	55	2	👊
★	Tauros	32	2	👊

ENERGY CARDS	# OF CARDS
Fire Energy	21
Double Colorless Energy	4

TRAINER CARDS	# OF CARDS
Professor Oak	1
Bill	2
Energy Retrieval	2
Poké Ball	1
Computer Search	1
Defender	2
Potion	3
Full Heal	1
Gambler	1
Recycle	3

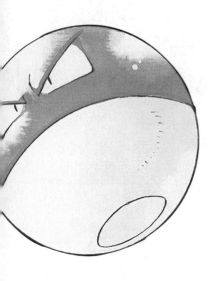

Water Medal
Autodeck Machine

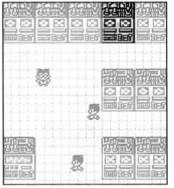

Medal: Water Medal
From: Amy 12

Remember that the Autodeck Machines don't give you cards and that they can work only with cards you already have. If you're missing cards needed for a specific deck, the machine will tell you what they are and how many you need. Some of the Water-type cards may be hard to come by, including Gyarados, Lapras, Articuno and Poliwrath.

Blue Water Deck

You won't have any energy problems with this Water-type-only deck, but with your Pokémon spread so thinly across so many evolutionary lines, you're going to have to rely mainly on basic creatures in combat. Focus! Focus!

TYPE	NAME	LEVEL	# OF CARDS	WEAKNESS
🌊	Psyduck	15	2	⚡
🌊	➤Golduck	27	1	⚡
🌊	Poliwag	13	2	🍃
🌊	➤Poliwhirl	28	1	🍃
🌊	➤Poliwrath	48	1	🍃
🌊	Seel	12	2	⚡
🌊	➤Dewgong	42	1	⚡
🌊	Shellder	8	2	⚡
🌊	➤Cloyster	25	1	⚡
🌊	Krabby	20	2	⚡
🌊	➤Kingler	27	1	⚡
🌊	Horsea	19	2	⚡
🌊	➤Seadra	23	1	⚡
🌊	Magikarp	8	1	⚡
🌊	➤Gyarados	41	1	🍃
🌊	➤Omanyte	19	1	🍃
🌊	➤Omastar	32	1	🍃
🌊	Lapras	31	1	⚡
🌊	Articuno	35	1	—

ENERGY CARDS	# OF CARDS
Water Energy	25
TRAINER CARDS	**# OF CARDS**
Professor Oak	1
Bill	2
Pokémon Trader	1
Mysterious Fossil	2
Energy Search	1
Poké Ball	1
Potion	1
Super Potion	1

On the Beach Deck

Sandshrew and Sandslash are here in case Electric-types come along to short-circuit the Water-types. If that's the case, maybe you shou[l] bump them up to four Sandshrew and three Sandslash and toss in a couple of Switch cards.

TYPE	NAME	LEVEL	# OF CARDS	WEAKNES[S]
🌊	Seel	12	2	⚡
🌊	➤Dewgong	42	1	⚡
🌊	Shellder	8	3	⚡
🌊	➤Cloyster	25	2	⚡
🌊	Krabby	20	3	⚡
🌊	➤Kingler	27	2	⚡
🌊	Staryu	15	3	⚡
🌊	➤Starmie	28	2	⚡
👊	Sandshrew	12	3	🍃
👊	➤Sandslash	33	2	🍃

ENERGY CARDS	# OF CARDS
Water Energy	16
Fighting Energy	10
TRAINER CARDS	**# OF CARDS**
Bill	2
Energy Retrieval	2
Energy Removal	2
Gust of Wind	2
Potion	3

Paralyze Deck

Of course, the purpose of this deck is to paralyze your enemies constantly, giving them no opportunity to retreat or fight back. If you'd rather not deal with a second Pokémon type, replace Caterpie and Metapod with more Water-types.

TYPE	NAME	LEVEL	# OF CARDS	WEAKNESS
⬢	Caterpie	13	3	🔥
⬢	►Metapod	21	2	🔥
💧	Squirtle	8	3	⚡
💧	►Wartortle	22	2	⚡
💧	Shellder	8	3	⚡
💧	►Cloyster	25	2	⚡
💧	Staryu	15	4	⚡
💧	►Starmie	28	3	⚡

ENERGY CARDS	# OF CARDS
Grass Energy	8
Water Energy	14
Double Colorless Energy	4

TRAINER CARDS	# OF CARDS
Professor Oak	2
Bill	2
PlusPower	2
Defender	2
Potion	4

Energy Removal Deck

We've advised limiting decks to two Pokémon types. You might make an exception if the third type is Colorless, since these Pokémon can use any energy. Try this deck, designed to steal your opponent's energy, and see what you think!

TYPE	NAME	LEVEL	# OF CARDS	WEAKNESS
💧	Psyduck	15	3	⚡
💧	►Golduck	27	2	⚡
💧	Poliwag	13	4	⬢
💧	►Poliwhirl	28	3	⬢
💧	►Poliwrath	48	2	⬢
👁	Gastly	17	4	—
👁	►Haunter	17	3	—
✦	Dratini	10	3	—
✦	►Dragonair	33	2	—

ENERGY CARDS	# OF CARDS
Water Energy	15
Psychic Energy	8
Double Colorless Energy	3

TRAINER CARDS	# OF CARDS
Professor Oak	1
Bill	1
Lass	1
Energy Search	2
Energy Removal	2
Super Energy Removal	1

Rain Dance Deck

With this deck, you can take advantage of a full range of Water-based powers, courtesy of Blastoise's Rain Dance ability. With it, you can play as many Water Energy Cards as you wish before your attack. There's no energy shortage here!

TYPE	NAME	LEVEL	# OF CARDS	WEAKNESS
💧	Squirtle	8	4	⚡
💧	►Wartortle	22	3	⚡
💧	►Blastoise	52	2	⚡
💧	Horsea	19	3	⚡
💧	►Seadra	23	2	⚡
💧	Goldeen	12	4	⚡
💧	►Seaking	28	3	⚡
💧	Lapras	31	2	⚡

ENERGY CARDS	# OF CARDS
Water Energy	24

TRAINER CARDS	# OF CARDS
Professor Oak	2
Pokémon Breeder	1
Energy Retrieval	1
Super Energy Retrieval	1
Energy Removal	2
Super Energy Removal	1
Switch	2
Potion	2
Gambler	1

Lightning Medal
Autodeck Machine

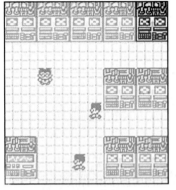

Medal: Lightning Medal
From: Isaac ⑯

We expect that a lot of you will enjoy these decks, as they feature everyone's favorite Pokémon, the lovable Pikachu. Plenty of other Lightning-type Pokémon have powers that are equally impressive, though, and you may find that some of them are even more useful in some combat situations. Don't believe us? Give these decks a whirl, and get back to us...

Cute Pokémon Deck

This should prove the old saying, "Looks aren't everything." Cute they may be, but these Pokémon have formidable powers. The only drawback is relying on so many basic creatures. Scoop Up, Mr. Fuji, Recycle and Defender can all help.

TYPE	NAME	LEVEL	# OF CARDS	WEAKNESS
⚡	Pikachu	12	1	👊
⚡	Pikachu	14	1	👊
⚡	Pikachu	16	1	👊
⚡	Pikachu	16	1	👊
⚡	Flying Pikachu	12	1	—
⚡	Surfing Pikachu	13	1	👊
⚡	Surfing Pikachu	13	1	👊
⚡	➤Raichu	40	1	👊
⚡	➤Raichu	45	1	👊
✴	Clefairy	14	2	👊
✴	➤Clefable	24	1	👊
✴	Jigglypuff	12	1	👊
✴	Jigglypuff	13	2	👊
✴	Jigglypuff	14	1	👊
✴	➤Wigglytuff	36	2	👊
✴	Eevee	12	4	👊
🔥	➤Flareon	28	1	💧
💧	➤Vaporeon	42	1	⚡
⚡	➤Jolteon	29	1	👊

ENERGY CARDS	# OF CARDS
Fire Energy	4
Water Energy	6
Lightning Energy	8
Double Colorless Energy	2

TRAINER CARDS	# OF CARDS
Professor Oak	2
Bill	3
Clefairy Doll	2
Scoop Up	2
Computer Search	1
PlusPower	1
Defender	1
Potion	3

Pokémon Flute Deck

Use Pokémon Flute to move a Pokémon from your foe's discard pile to his or her Bench, then use Gust of Wind to shove it into the arena. If you go with the flute strategy, you should also use Pokémon that can attack your opponent's Bench.

TYPE	NAME	LEVEL	# OF CARDS	WEAKNES
⚡	Pikachu	12	3	👊
⚡	➤Raichu	40	1	👊
✴	Rattata	9	2	👊
✴	➤Raticate	41	1	👊
💧	Staryu	15	2	⚡
💧	Lapras	31	2	⚡
⚡	Magnemite	13	2	👊
⚡	Electabuzz	32	3	👊

ENERGY CARDS	# OF CARDS
Water Energy	9
Lightning Energy	12

TRAINER CARDS	# OF CARDS
Professor Oak	2
Bill	4
Energy Removal	3
Computer Search	1
PlusPower	3
Item Finder	2
Gust of Wind	4
Pokémon Flute	4

Yellow Flash Deck

As you can see, you don't always have to use the same version of a creature, for example, using a level-12 and a level-14 Pikachu. Sometimes being inconsistent in your attacks is good, if only to keep your opponent guessing.

TYPE	NAME	LEVEL	# OF CARDS	WEAKNESS
⚡	Pikachu	12	2	✊
⚡	Pikachu	14	1	✊
⚡	►Raichu	40	1	✊
⚡	►Raichu	45	1	✊
⚡	Magnemite	13	2	✊
⚡	Magnemite	15	1	✊
⚡	►Magneton	28	1	✊
⚡	►Magneton	35	1	✊
⚡	Voltorb	10	3	✊
⚡	►Electrode	35	1	✊
⚡	►Electrode	42	1	✊
★	Eevee	12	3	✊
⚡	►Jolteon	24	1	✊
⚡	►Jolteon	29	1	✊
⚡	Electabuzz	20	1	✊
⚡	Electabuzz	35	1	✊
⚡	Zapdos	40	1	—
⚡	Zapdos	64	1	—

ENERGY CARDS	# OF CARDS
Lightning Energy	26
TRAINER CARDS	# OF CARDS
Energy Retrieval	1
Energy Removal	2
Poké Ball	2
PlusPower	2
Defender	2
Gust of Wind	1

Electric Shock Deck

Porygon makes an effective wall while you evolve the Pokémon on your Bench. When you're ready, use a Switch Card (you'll have to add a few to the deck) to put one of your heavy hitters into the arena. Talk about hair raising!

TYPE	NAME	LEVEL	# OF CARDS	WEAKNESS
⚡	Pikachu	14	2	✊
⚡	Pikachu	16	1	✊
⚡	Pikachu	16	1	✊
⚡	►Raichu	40	2	✊
⚡	Magnemite	13	2	✊
⚡	Magnemite	15	2	✊
⚡	►Magneton	28	2	✊
⚡	Voltorb	10	4	✊
⚡	►Electrode	42	3	✊
⚡	Zapdos	64	1	—
★	Porygon	12	3	✊

ENERGY CARDS	# OF CARDS
Lightning Energy	24
Double Colorless Energy	1
TRAINER CARDS	# OF CARDS
Energy Retrieval	2
PlusPower	2
Defender	3
Item Finder	2
Gust of Wind	3

Zapping Self-Destruct Deck

The strategy here is exactly what you think it is: Blow up your own Pokémon. Defender Cards can help your Pokémon survive the explosions, and in case they don't, stock up on Energy Retrieval and Recycle Cards. You'll be glad you did.

TYPE	NAME	LEVEL	# OF CARDS	WEAKNESS
⚡	Magnemite	13	4	✊
⚡	►Magneton	28	3	✊
⚡	Voltorb	10	4	✊
⚡	►Electrode	35	2	✊
⚡	Electabuzz	35	4	✊
★	Kangaskhan	40	2	✊
★	Tauros	32	1	✊

ENERGY CARDS	# OF CARDS
Lightning Energy	24
Double Colorless Energy	2
TRAINER CARDS	# OF CARDS
Professor Oak	1
Bill	2
Switch	2
Defender	4
Gust of Wind	1
Potion	4

Science Medal
Autodeck Machine

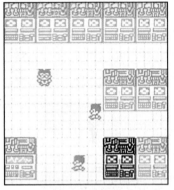

Medal: Science Medal
From: Rick 🔘**20**

The Science decks use mainly Grass-type Pokémon, backed by a smattering of Colorless, Psychic and Lightning-type comrades. Ironically, some of these decks look more Grass-oriented than the Grass decks, but remember that these scientific creatures often have powers outside the usual poison, paralyze and sleep effects you usually see in Grass-types.

Lovely Nidoran Deck

Here's a clever twist on the old Call for Family tactic. With basic Nidoran♀ or Nidoran♂ in play, use Pokémon Trader to bring their Stage 2 Cards to your hand, and then use Pokémon Breeder to play them directly on your basics.

TYPE	NAME	LEVEL	# OF CARDS	WEAKNESS
🍃	Nidoran♀	13	4	👁
🍃	➤Nidorina	24	3	👁
🍃	➤Nidoqueen	43	2	👁
🍃	Nidoran♂	20	4	👁
🍃	➤Nidorino	25	4	👁
🍃	➤Nidoking	48	4	👁
★	Lickitung	26	3	👊

ENERGY CARDS	# OF CARDS
Grass Energy	20

TRAINER CARDS	# OF CARDS
Professor Oak	2
Pokémon Trader	3
Pokémon Breeder	3
Energy Retrieval	2
Switch	3
Computer Search	1
Item Finder	2

Science Corps Deck

Once again, we're presented with a deck with lots of power but little purpose. Pick and choose from your favorite special effect attacks and chuck the rest. The mix of Trainer Cards also needs help—look at all those singles!

TYPE	NAME	LEVEL	# OF CARDS	WEAKNESS
🍃	Ekans	10	2	👁
🍃	➤Arbok	27	1	👁
🍃	Nidoran♀	13	2	👁
🍃	➤Nidorina	24	1	👁
🍃	➤Nidoqueen	43	1	👁
🍃	Nidoran♂	20	3	👁
🍃	➤Nidorino	25	2	👁
🍃	➤Nidoking	48	1	👁
🍃	Zubat	10	2	👁
🍃	➤Golbat	29	1	👁
🍃	Grimer	17	2	👁
🍃	➤Muk	34	1	👁
🍃	Koffing	13	2	👁
🍃	➤Weezing	27	1	👁
★	Meowth	15	2	👊
★	➤Persian	25	1	👊

ENERGY CARDS	# OF CARDS
Grass Energy	26

TRAINER CARDS	# OF CARDS
Professor Oak	1
Bill	1
Pokémon Trader	1
Pokémon Breeder	1
Potion	1
Full Heal	1
Maintenance	1
Gambler	1
Recycle	1

Flyin' Pokémon Deck

With its Colorless-and-Flying-types, this deck is aimed squarely at Fighting-types, but it lacks focus. Do you prefer damage prevention/healing (Golbat and Fearow) or disrupting your foe's hand (level-40 Pidgeot + Imposter Prof. Oak)?

TYPE	NAME	LEVEL	# OF CARDS	WEAKNESS
🌿	Zubat	10	4	👁
🌿	➤Golbat	29	3	👁
✸	Pidgey	8	4	⚡
✸	➤Pidgeotto	36	3	⚡
✸	➤Pidgeot	38	1	⚡
✸	➤Pidgeot	40	1	⚡
✸	Spearow	13	4	⚡
✸	➤Fearow	27	3	⚡
⚡	Flying Pikachu	12	2	—

ENERGY CARDS	# OF CARDS
Grass Energy	13
Lightning Energy	10
Double Colorless Energy	2

TRAINER CARDS	# OF CARDS
Imposter Professor Oak	2
Bill	2
Lass	2
Potion	4

Poison Deck

Do we really need to explain the object here? Didn't think so. Just tighten up the mix of Trainer Cards a bit—you'll be ready to roll. Energy Removal could prevent a poisoned opponent from retreating to the safety of the Bench...

TYPE	NAME	LEVEL	# OF CARDS	WEAKNESS
🌿	Weedle	12	3	🔥
🌿	➤Kakuna	23	2	🔥
🌿	➤Beedrill	32	1	🔥
🌿	Ekans	10	4	👁
🌿	➤Arbok	27	3	👁
🌿	Nidoran♂	20	4	👁
🌿	➤Nidorino	25	3	👁
🌿	➤Nidoking	48	2	👁
🌿	Koffing	13	3	👁
🌿	➤Weezing	27	2	👁

ENERGY CARDS	# OF CARDS
Grass Energy	24

TRAINER CARDS	# OF CARDS
Professor Oak	1
Imposter Professor Oak	2
Pokémon Breeder	1
Potion	2
Full Heal	2
Gambler	1

Wonders of Science Deck

Once again, this deck seems to be more of an interesting base on which to build, rather than a finished deck. Using Pokémon with comparatively low HP, you'll have to strike early and strike first to better your chances of winning.

TYPE	NAME	LEVEL	# OF CARDS	WEAKNESS
🌿	Grimer	17	4	👁
🌿	➤Muk	34	3	👁
🌿	Koffing	13	4	👁
🌿	➤Weezing	27	3	👁
👁	Mewtwo	53	2	👁
👁	Mewtwo	60	1	👁
👁	Mewtwo	60	1	👁
✸	Porygon	12	2	👊

ENERGY CARDS	# OF CARDS
Grass Energy	15
Psychic Energy	8

TRAINER CARDS	# OF CARDS
Professor Oak	2
Imposter Professor Oak	1
Bill	2
Energy Search	2
Switch	2
Computer Search	2
Pokédex	2
Full Heal	2
Maintenance	2

Psychic Medal
Autodeck Machine

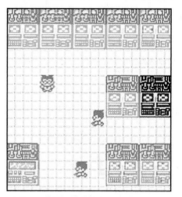

Medal: Psychic Medal
From: Murray **24**

There's no such thing as a foolproof deck, but you can be pretty darn close with a Psychic-type deck. Psychic-types have weaknesses only to themselves and a few regular Fighting-types, so they have a natural strength that can be tough for opponents to overcome. After you give them a test drive, these decks may become some of your favorites.

Psychic Power Deck

This deck is a Psychic smorgasbord, crammed with some of the major mental powers in the game. Treat it like any buffet: Take what you want and leave the rest. Oh, and don't forget to beef up your selection of Trainer Cards.

TYPE	NAME	LEVEL	# OF CARDS	WEAKNESS
👁	Abra	10	3	👁
👁	▶Kadabra	38	2	👁
👁	▶Alakazam	42	1	👁
👁	Slowpoke	18	2	👁
👁	▶Slowbro	26	1	👁
👁	Gastly	8	1	—
👁	Gastly	17	2	—
👁	▶Haunter	17	1	—
👁	▶Haunter	22	1	—
👁	▶Gengar	38	1	—
👁	Drowzee	12	2	👁
👁	▶Hypno	36	1	👁
✶	Clefairy	14	1	👊
✶	▶Clefable	34	1	👊
👁	Mr. Mime	28	1	👁
👁	Jynx	23	1	👁
✶	Snorlax	20	1	👊
👁	Mewtwo	53	1	👁
👁	Mew	23	1	👁

ENERGY CARDS	# OF CARDS
Psychic Energy	25

TRAINER CARDS	# OF CARDS
Professor Oak	2
Pokémon Trader	1
PlusPower	2
Pokémon Breeder	1
Switch	2
Pokémon Center	1
Devolution Spray	1

Dream Eater Haunter Deck

Haunter has top billing in this deck, but it's not the major player. You should focus more on Gengar and Hypno, with their matching Dark Mind abilities. Revive doesn't seem to have much purpose here; try Gust of Wind instead.

TYPE	NAME	LEVEL	# OF CARDS	WEAKNESS
🍃	Zubat	10	3	👁
⚡	▶Golbat	29	2	👁
👁	Gastly	8	4	—
👁	▶Haunter	17	1	—
👁	▶Haunter	22	2	—
👁	▶Gengar	38	2	—
👁	Drowzee	12	3	👁
👁	▶Hypno	36	2	👁
✶	Jigglypuff	14	2	👊
✶	Meowth	15	2	👊

ENERGY CARDS	# OF CARDS
Grass Energy	7
Psychic Energy	17

TRAINER CARDS	# OF CARDS
Professor Oak	2
Bill	2
Energy Retrieval	2
Super Energy Retrieval	1
Switch	2
Computer Search	1
Revive	3

Scavenging Slowbro Deck

Here's a sneaky trick we haven't tried before. Use Slowbro's Strange Behavior power to absorb its comrades' damage, then use Mew's Devolution Beam to return Slowbro to your hand. Slowbro will be healed and ready to rock again!

TYPE	NAME	LEVEL	# OF CARDS	WEAKNESS
◉	Slowpoke	18	4	◉
◉	→Slowbro	26	3	◉
✶	Jigglypuff	13	2	✊
✶	Jigglypuff	14	2	✊
✶	Eevee	12	2	✊
◉	Jynx	23	3	◉
◉	Mewtwo	53	2	◉
◉	Mew	23	2	◉

ENERGY CARDS	# OF CARDS
Psychic Energy	23

TRAINER CARDS	# OF CARDS
Energy Retrieval	2
Energy Removal	3
PlusPower	2
Defender	3
Potion	3
Recycle	4

Strange Power Deck

This deck seems to work much the same as the previous one, but the addition of Hypno gives you the ability to strike your foe's Bench. Once again, though, your Trainer Cards seem woefully scattered and unfocused.

TYPE	NAME	LEVEL	# OF CARDS	WEAKNESS
◉	Slowpoke	9	3	◉
◉	→Slowbro	26	2	◉
◉	Drowzee	12	4	◉
◉	→Hypno	36	3	◉
◉	Mr. Mime	28	2	◉
◉	Jynx	23	2	◉
✶	Lickitung	26	2	✊
✶	Snorlax	20	1	✊
◉	Mew	8	1	◉
◉	Mew	23	2	◉

ENERGY CARDS	# OF CARDS
Psychic Energy	25
Double Colorless Energy	1

TRAINER CARDS	# OF CARDS
Pokémon Trader	2
Energy Retrieval	2
Energy Removal	2
Super Energy Removal	1
PlusPower	2
Item Finder	1
Gust of wind	1
Full Heal	1

Strange Psyshock Deck

Use Alakazam's Damage Swap to move damage counters to Pokémon with no energy, and then use Pokémon Center to heal them free of charge! Of course, you should add two more Pokémon Centers to this deck before you use it.

TYPE	NAME	LEVEL	# OF CARDS	WEAKNESS
◉	Abra	10	4	◉
◉	→Kadabra	38	3	◉
◉	→Alakazam	42	2	◉
◉	Mr. Mime	28	2	◉
✶	Chansey	55	3	✊
✶	Kangaskhan	40	3	✊
✶	Snorlax	20	2	✊

ENERGY CARDS	# OF CARDS
Psychic Energy	22

TRAINER CARDS	# OF CARDS
Professor Oak	2
Energy Removal	3
Switch	4
Pokémon Center	2
Scoop Up	4
Gust of Wind	3
Gambler	1

Fighting Medal
Autodeck Machine

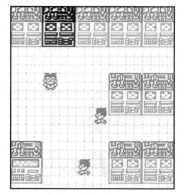

Medal: Fighting Medal
From: Mitch 28

What Fighting-type Pokémon lack in fancy powers they more than make up with in fancy footwork and powerful punches. They're a great addition in many two-type decks, with other Pokémon creating the openings and the Fighting-types delivering the K.O.s. They often have relatively low energy costs, which is another terrific plus.

All Fighting Deck

It seems that most every machine must have a "buffet" deck, trotting out practically every Pokémon of that type. This is your chance to compare the Fighting-types and see which ones fit your play style or current strategies.

TYPE	NAME	LEVEL	# OF CARDS	WEAKNESS
👊	Sandshrew	12	2	🍃
👊	▶ Sandslash	33	1	🍃
👊	Diglett	8	2	🍃
👊	▶ Dugtrio	36	1	🍃
👊	Mankey	7	2	👁
👊	▶ Primeape	35	1	👁
👊	Machop	20	3	👁
👊	▶ Machoke	40	2	👁
👊	▶ Machamp	67	1	👁
👊	Geodude	16	2	🍃
👊	▶ Graveler	29	1	🍃
👊	▶ Golem	36	1	🍃
👊	Cubone	13	2	🍃
👊	▶ Marowak	26	1	🍃
👊	Rhyhorn	18	2	🍃
👊	▶ Rhydon	48	1	🍃
👊	Onix	12	1	🍃
👊	Hitmonlee	30	1	👁
👊	Hitmonchan	33	1	👁

ENERGY CARDS	# OF CARDS
Fighting Energy	26

TRAINER CARDS	# OF CARDS
Professor Oak	1
Bill	2
Switch	1
Potion	2

Bench Attack Deck

As you might expect, this deck is targeted at your opponent's benched Pokémon. Defender will help the "remote control" strikers, like Hitmonlee, as well as the self-destructing Electrode. A few Mr. Fuji Cards wouldn't hurt, either.

TYPE	NAME	LEVEL	# OF CARDS	WEAKNESS
⚡	Voltorb	10	4	👊
⚡	▶ Electrode	42	2	👊
⚡	Zapdos	40	2	—
👊	Hitmonlee	30	4	👁
👊	Hitmonchan	33	2	👁
★	Meowth	14	4	👊

ENERGY CARDS	# OF CARDS
Lightning Energy	12
Fighting Energy	14

TRAINER CARDS	# OF CARDS
Professor Oak	1
Bill	2
Mr. Fuji	1
Energy Retrieval	2
Switch	2
Scoop Up	1
PlusPower	2
Defender	2
Item Finder	1
Gust of Wind	1
Maintenance	1